RETURN TO
TITLETOWN

The Remarkable Story *of the*
2010 Green Bay Packers

Text by Chuck Carlson

TRIUMPH
BOOKS

Packers coach Mike McCarthy hoists the Vince Lombardi Trophy after the Packers defeated the Pittsburgh Steelers in Super Bowl XLV.

This book is available in quantity at special discounts for your group or organization. For further information contact:

Triumph Books
542 South Dearborn Street
Suite 750
Chicago, IL 60605
Phone: (312) 939-3330
Fax: (312) 663-3557
www.triumphbooks.com

Printed in the United States of America
ISBN: 978-1-60078-641-9

Content packaged by Mojo Media, Inc.
Joe Funk: Editor
Jason Hinman: Creative Director

All interior photographs courtesy of AP Images

Front cover photo by Ronald Martinez/Getty Images
Back cover photo courtesy of AP Images

contents

A Season to Remember

There are teams that have an aura about them. You look at them and you know as well as you know your own name that they are destined for greatness—sometimes before a single game has even been played. They have the players, the attitude, the mentality, the certain indefinable something that says something is special in this group's DNA.

This was not what you necessarily saw with the 2010 Green Bay Packers.

Yes, the team had talent and many of the pieces seemed to be in place for a run at the Super Bowl.

But there were nagging, unsettling questions about this bunch as early as January 2010 when they lost a surreal 51–45 NFC playoff game to the Arizona Cardinals.

As the 2010 regular season dawned, the doubters—and there were plenty—didn't trust the Packers defense or head coach Mike McCarthy or the play of talented-but-inconsistent quarterback Aaron Rodgers.

But the Packers answered all those questions and a few more. The defense, under the brilliant guidance of Dom Capers, was one of the best in the NFL. McCarthy made superb adjustments. Rodgers continued his evolution as one of the game's top quarterbacks, causing Packers fans to almost forget about the guy who had previously been under center, good old what's-his-name.

This team had an internal toughness no one expected. The Packers suffered through the kind of injury plague that would have destroyed other teams. Starters like Nick Barnett, Jermichael Finley, Ryan Grant, Brandon Chillar,

Mark Tauscher, and Morgan Burnett missed much of the season. Key backups like Mike Neal, Brady Poppinga, Derrick Martin, Spencer Havner, and Justin Harrell were lost, too. In all, the Packers placed 15 players on the injured reserve list. It was an incredible run of bad luck, and the Packers handled it all.

To look for a turning point in this remarkable season would be a waste of time. There was no real place where the light switch went on and everything fell into place. It was a season of fits and starts, of horrendous performances and breathtaking comebacks. It was a season that saw the Packers rout the Dallas Cowboys and New York Giants but lose to the Detroit Lions and Washington Redskins.

It was a season that came down to this: win your last two games of the regular season or face the crushing disappointment of missing the playoffs with a team that was too good to stay home.

The Packers did all that and maybe a little bit more, winning three straight playoff games on the road, two against teams they had already lost to during the season.

These Packers are schooled in the history and legacy of this organization. They all tour the Packers Hall of Fame and know about Curly Lambeau, Vince Lombardi, Paul Hornung, Don Hutson, and the Packer Sweep as well as—yes—Brett Favre.

By doing what it has done this season, this team added to the legend of the Green Bay Packers, and they have written their own special chapter in a book that no one will ever get tired of reading. ■

Aaron Rodgers was all smiles after leading the Packers to victory in Super Bowl XLV.

The Pack Is Back

February 6, 2011 • Cowboys Stadium, Arlington, Texas

It was their season in small. For four gut-wrenching hours, the Green Bay Packers, as they had done in September and October and November and December and January, found a way to prevail. It was not with anything resembling grace or ease or comfort, but these Packers would have had it no other way.

In Super Bowl XLV in front of nearly 103,000 people in frozen North Texas, the Packers again overcame the same debilitating injuries that tested them all season and won their fourth Lombardi Trophy.

The sixth and final seed in the NFC playoffs; the second-youngest team in the NFL; the team which placed 15 players on the injured reserve list; the team that most people had given up for dead with two weeks left in the season came through one more time and did what no one really expected.

Aaron Rodgers, who three years earlier was booed and reviled for taking over the quarterback spot from a legend, completed 24 of 39 passes for 304 yards and three scores and was named the game's MVP as the Packers won their fourth Super Bowl and 13th world title.

And when it was over, the Cowboys Stadium crowd, which was dominated by Packers fans, chanted their familiar mantra "Go, Pack, Go!"

It was the sublime conclusion to an unforgettable season.

"They're the best fans in the league," Rodgers said. "The Lombardi Trophy is coming back to Titletown."

Packers 31, Steelers 25

	1	2	3	4	F
PIT	0	10	7	8	25
GB	14	7	0	10	31

9 The number of catches wide receiver Jordy Nelson made in the game, including a 38-yard touchdown.

Coach Mike McCarthy, who had absorbed his share of criticism over the years for being an erratic play-caller, could only beam afterward.

"This is what you work for," he said. "I can't give our players enough credit. We had bumps in the road but we kept fighting. It was a great team victory."

Asked about returning to Green Bay with the Lombardi Trophy, named for legendary Packers coach Vince Lombardi, McCarthy said simply. "I feel like I'm doing my job."

It was a game that saw the Pittsburgh Steelers, with 25 players who had competed on the Steelers' last Super Bowl team just two years ago, facing a Packers team with only two players (cornerback Charles Woodson and nose tackle Ryan Pickett) who had ever played on this stage before.

Aaron Rodgers releases a pass under pressure from Steelers linebacker James Harrison. Rodgers was named the MVP of Super Bowl XLV after throwing for 304 yards and three touchdowns.

But it was the Packers, despite the two weeks of hype and Super Bowl silliness, that came out calmer and more prepared to play.

The Packers struck first late in the first quarter as Rodgers drove the Packers 80 yards in nine plays. There was nothing flashy about this typical, workmanlike Packers drive. Running back James Starks, a seventh-round draft pick who had missed much of the season with injury and inconsistency but emerged as a playoff force, had three big carries for 17 yards, including a rugged 8-yard run on third down and 1. Rodgers then capped the drive with a perfect 29-yard touchdown pass to Jordy Nelson.

The first score was huge and set the tone. The Packers made it clear early that they were not intimidated by the setting or the situation, while the Steelers misfired early and committed bad penalties.

One of the mistakes was especially disastrous for the Steelers, who are now 6–2 in Super Bowls.

On the Steelers next offensive play after the Green Bay score, quarterback Ben Roethlisberger's arm was hit by backup nose tackle Howard Green and his pass fluttered toward the left sideline to seemingly no one in particular.

(above) Jordy Nelson was a key player from early on, finishing with nine catches for 140 yards and a touchdown.
(opposite) Greg Jennings catches an 8-yard touchdown pass from Aaron Rodgers in the fourth quarter to give the Packers a 28–17 lead.

Packers safety Nick Collins dives into the end zone, completing a 37-yard interception return for a touchdown in the first quarter to give the Packers a 14–0 lead.

But Packers cornerback Nick Collins closed on the ball, picked it off, and bounced and winded his way 37 yards, diving into the end zone for a stunning 14–0 lead.

Asked what he was thinking as he saw the ball come to him, Collins said simply, "I had to make sure I caught the ball. And I wanted to get to the end zone; I had to get to the end zone."

After a Steelers field goal cut the deficit to 14–3, the Packers defense again made a huge play as backup cornerback Jarrett Bush jumped in front of a Roethlisberger pass for his first interception of the season at the Green Bay 47.

"There were a lot of throws I wished I had back," said Roethlisberger, who had won two Super Bowls as Pittsburgh's starting quarterback.

Rodgers followed that turnover with completions of 4 yards to Greg Jennings and 16 to Nelson before Starks ripped off a 12-yard run.

Now thoroughly back on its heels, the Steelers defense could only watch as Rodgers rifled a pass over the middle to Jennings, a pass thrown so hard he dislocated Jennings' ring finger. But Jennings hung on to the ball despite a big hit and the Packers had a 21–3 lead.

But the Packers knew it wouldn't be that easy and, of course, it wasn't.

In a series that turned the game in more ways than one, the Steelers finally got in gear offensively.

On first and 10 from their own 23, Roethlisberger threw 37 yards to Antwaan Randle El on a play that injured Packers cornerback Sam Shields and sent him to the locker room.

On the next play, Roethlisberger tried to connect with Wallace down the left sideline but as he dove for the ball, so did Packers veteran cornerback and defensive backbone Charles Woodson. Woodson landed awkwardly on his left side and he too left the game, favoring his left shoulder.

Down two key elements in the secondary, the Steelers scored with 39 seconds left in the half when Roethlisberger connected with Hines Ward for a critical, momentum-shifting touchdown.

Though leading 21–10 at the half, the Packers received a thunderbolt in their locker room—Woodson had a broken collarbone and was done for the game. That wasn't all: veteran wide receiver Donald Driver injured his

Clay Matthews tackles Ben Roethlisberger during the first half. Under pressure all game, the Steelers quarterback threw two interceptions and completed 25 of 40 passes.

ankle and was out for the rest of the game as well.

What else was new? It was two more catastrophic injuries for a team that absorbed more than its share all season.

Woodson's loss was especially damaging because he was the defensive wildcard, the guy who could play against top receivers but could also rush the quarterback and play great run defense.

"I've broken a few things in my time and I knew it was broken," Woodson said later of his collarbone.

Knowing he was sidelined the rest of the night, Woodson tried to address his teammates before they went back on the field. And after telling them how much this game meant to him and to go out and play hard, he broke down crying.

"I haven't cried that hard since I was a kid," Woodson said.

"He couldn't even get the words out," Collins said afterward. "It was hard for him. It was hard for everyone."

The Packers were intent to go back out and win it for their two veterans—Woodson and Driver, who between them had 25 years of NFL experience.

But the Packers were clearly off kilter in the third quarter, committing two penalties on their first three plays, followed by a dropped pass by James Jones that probably would have resulted in a touchdown.

After another Packers penalty on a punt, the Steelers only had to drive 50 yards, all on the ground, for an 8-yard Rashard Mendenhall touchdown.

Momentum was clearly on Pittsburgh's side and it continued when the Packers did nothing on their next possession. The Steelers moved again on offense, driving to the Packers 29 before the defense finally woke up and played the way it was expected to play. A pass to Heath Miller lost two yards and then linebacker Frank Zombo sacked Roethlisberger.

Shaun Suisham's 52-yard field goal attempt wasn't even close and the Packers survived another Steelers hay-maker. It was a third quarter from hell for the Packers offensively but, somehow, they were still ahead 21–17.

Then came the final turning point of Super Bowl XLV. On first and 10 from the Packers 33, Mendenhall was hit by linebacker Clay Matthews and fumbled. Fellow linebacker Desmond Bishop, another player who stepped in when injuries struck, scooped up the loose ball and returned it to the Green Bay 45.

Aaron Rodgers lets a pass loose during the second half.

Cornerback Charles Woodson breaks up a pass intended for Steelers receiver Mike Wallace during the second quarter. Woodson broke his collarbone when he hit the Cowboys Stadium turf and did not return to the game.

On a key third down from the Steelers 40, Rodgers hit Nelson, who had a dropped a pass on the previous down, on a crossing pattern for 38 yards. Two plays later, Rodgers connected with Jennings for the touchdown and a 28–17 cushion with 12:03 to play. But that wouldn't last long.

Pittsburgh came right back, driving 70 yards on seven plays and ending the drive by finding Wallace for the 25-yard score. The two-point conversion cut the Packers' lead to 28–25 with more than seven minutes to play.

All Rodgers did was respond with what may go down as one of the best drives in Packers history—and it didn't even result in a touchdown.

He went from his own 25 to the Steelers 5, taking more than five crucial minutes off the clock. The key play came on third and 10 from the Green Bay 25 when Rodgers threw a perfect pass to Jennings for 31 yards.

The drive eventually bogged down but Mason Crosby still kicked a 23-yard field goal with 2:10 to play.

"We needed a drive there," Rodgers said. "I wish we could have finished it with seven points, but we got the job done."

Now the Steelers needed a touchdown to win and Roethlisberger was just the guy to pull off a Super Bowl miracle, just as he done two years earlier in beating the Arizona Cardinals. But it wasn't to be.

After gaining one first down, Roethlisberger threw three straight incompletions, the last bouncing off Wallace's

(above) Packers coach Mike McCarthy receives a Gatorade shower from tackle T.J. Lang. (opposite) Packers veteran receiver Donald Driver, who injured his ankle in the second quarter, kisses the Vince Lombardi Trophy after Super Bowl XLV.

hands, who desperately sought a pass interference call.

After the final pass hit the ground, Rodgers raised his arms, smiled, and looked behind him.

"I was looking for someone to hug but I didn't know what to do," Rodgers said later.

Rodgers was impeccable, especially in the second half when the offense was struggling. All he did when the Packers needed a sustained drive was come up with one.

"We put this game on his shoulders from a game play standpoint and he delivered," McCarthy said.

"He's going to be an elite quarterback in this league for years," Matthews said.

Rodgers, as he'd been all season, was cool and collected despite the huge stage. Indeed, of Rodgers' 15 incompletions, six were dropped passes. He is also just one of four Super Bowl quarterbacks to throw for three touchdowns and 300 yards, and only two of those—his boyhood heroes Joe Montana and Steve Young—did it in victory.

"I felt pretty good tonight," Rodgers said. "I had a pretty good week of preparation and Mike was rolling through his plays. It was an incredible feeling."

For the Packers, it was the exclamation mark to a season that saw as many lows as highs. It was also a team that saw player after player step into situations where few figured they could be successful. These Packers were just the second No. 6 seed, joining the 2005 Steelers, to win a Super Bowl.

"We have great character guys here," linebacker A.J. Hawk said. "You just stay the course. I know it's a cliché but that's the way it is."

Said Collins: "We just get along real well as a team. We play as one unit. We don't have a bunch of individuals. We have guys who love to play football for 60 minutes."

So now the talk goes inevitably to whether the Packers can repeat. Remember, they won the Super Bowl without their top running back, two of their best linebackers, and their best tight end.

This could be a team built for the long haul.

Rodgers just smiled when asked about the Packers' future.

"We have a lot of high-character men," he said. "We can win with the guys in this locker room."

Indeed they can. ∎

As confetti flies from the ceiling, Aaron Rodgers—with a pro wrestling championship belt on his shoulder—and Clay Matthews celebrate after Super Bowl XLV.

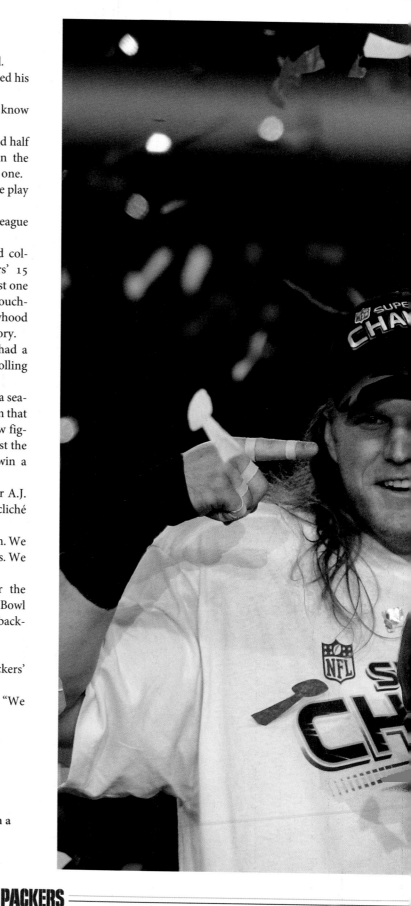

Ted Thompson

Architect of a Championship Squad

Do not expect wonderful pronouncements from the man who built these Green Bay Packers. Ted Thompson is not quotable, and he is not memorable. And that's exactly the way he wants it. Indeed, if 50 words are required to make a point, he'd rather say five. Actually, he'd rather say nothing at all.

"It's not about me," Thompson says softly.

He says everything softly.

But make no mistake: Thompson may not say much but there is plenty going on under the surface. He is smart, uncompromising, and, when required, as ruthless as the day is long.

He has orchestrated some of the most controversial moves in team history, incurring the wrath of many Packers fans, some of whom have called for his firing almost since the day he was hired.

He let standouts like kicker Ryan Longwell, safety Darren Sharper, and center Mike Flanagan leave through free agency because he was convinced they could be replaced for less money. He refused to be swayed by the vagaries of free agency, declining to get into bidding wars for high-priced players who might not fit the style, image, or design of the team he had in mind. He took his share of heat for that, too.

Ted Thompson was born to be an NFL general manager the way some men are born to be soldiers or florists or poets. He has been a football guy his entire life—first as a nondescript player for the Houston Oilers and then on the personnel side, learning at the side of Ron Wolf as he was building the Packers into a powerhouse in the 1990s.

In 2000, when Mike Holmgren left the Packers to take over as GM/head coach of the Seattle Seahawks, Thompson went with him as director of pro personnel. In January 2005, after five years in Seattle, Thompson was named Packers general manager, taking the role away from Mike Sherman, who would serve simply as head coach for a long, uncomfortable year.

One of Thompson's first acts for the Packers was the 2005 NFL Draft when—mostly due to the short-sightedness of several teams—quarterback Aaron Rodgers went undrafted until late in the first round. Thompson snapped him up, convinced he was the Packers quarterback of the future once Brett Favre decided to retire. In the next round, he took an unknown safety from Bethune-Cookman, Nick Collins, who has since taken his place as one of the best safeties in football.

The following year, after the Packers tumbled to 4–12, their worst record in 14 years, Thompson replaced the unhappy Sherman with Mike McCarthy.

"This was more thinking in terms of where we are and where we need to get to," Thompson said in his usual understated fashion.

In the years that followed, Thompson continued to build the Packers in a way he was convinced would be successful

In an organization blessed with many talented decision-makers, Ted Thompson deserves the bulk of the credit for assembling the Super Bowl XLV squad.

not only on the field but which would not wreck the franchise financially down the road. Indeed, for three years, the Packers were the youngest team in football as Thompson added and subtracted pieces as he felt necessary.

Thompson landed squarely in the crosshairs of rabid Packers fans in the spring of 2008 when Favre, sensing the Packers were looking farther down the road than he was, decided to retire. Taking his cue, the Packers thanked Favre for his years of service and gave the starting quarterback job to Rodgers.

A few months later, Favre changed his mind and asked for his job back, a move Thompson was unwilling to make. In a bizarre dance of battling wills, McCarthy, Thompson, and Favre all gathered for a day-long meeting that eventually resulted in an unhappy Favre departing Green Bay. A few days later he was traded to the New York Jets.

Favre and Thompson have not spoken since.

Because of his distaste for playing events out in public, Thompson never really explained his decision, leaving fans and other observers perplexed.

As it turned out, Thompson knew exactly what he was doing. Rodgers grabbed the starting job and has flourished since. Thompson has continued to build the Packers team he originally envisioned—drafting young stars like A.J. Hawk, Greg Jennings, Jermichael Finley, B.J. Raji, and Clay Matthews and complementing them with young free agents.

It's possible that Thompson never will be loved by demanding Packers fans. He is too distant, too analytical, too bloodless for that. But respect? That's another story.

In fact, on a popular Packers website called "Fire Ted Thompson Now" is this updated message from the owner—"I'm Not Afraid to Admit It. I Was Wrong. Congrats Ted."

That says it all. ∎

Mike McCarthy, Mark Murphy, and Ted Thompson are calm, cool, and collected in the Packers "war room" at the kickoff of the 2010 NFL Draft.

A Major Vick-tory

September 12, 2010 • Lincoln Financial Field, Philadelphia, Pennsylvania

Everything the Green Bay Packers would be in 2010, they would introduce in the first, rugged game of the season. That first contest against the Philadelphia Eagles was, in a very real sense, a microcosm of the entire season.

The opener of a wild 16-game campaign revealed the Packers' tough defense, led by a flowing-haired madman linebacker named Clay Matthews. They debuted an offense that could be breathtaking one minute and stunningly inert the next. They made plays one minute and no plays the next.

And they suffered shattering, debilitating injuries to key players that were seemingly impossible to recover from.

But at Philly's Lincoln Financial Field, the Packers hopped on board their Super Bowl Express and took the first in many winding, twisting turns. It would not be easy. But what else was new?

Already the preseason favorite of many to reach the Super Bowl, the Packers had to start their quest in a city in which they hadn't won in more than four decades. And they made a quick, early statement when Matthews, the second-year linebacker from Southern California with an impeccable NFL pedigree, knocked out the Eagles' presumptive starting quarterback, Kevin Kolb, with a first-half concussion.

The Packers led the Eagles 13–3 at halftime when Philadelphia coach Andy Reid replaced the ailing Kolb with his backup, the mercurial Michael Vick. It altered the

Packers 27, Eagles 20

	1	2	3	4	F
GB	0	13	14	0	27
PHI	3	0	7	10	20

56 Yardage of Mason Crosby's second-quarter field goal, a Packers record

game and forced the Packers' defense into a role it hadn't anticipated.

Mobile and dangerous, Vick, who had missed two full seasons because of a federal dog abuse conviction and sat for most of the '09 season behind Donovan McNabb, used his legs and his arm to cause Green Bay fits.

The Eagles trailed 27–10 after three quarters but clawed to within 27–20 with five minutes to play thanks mostly to Vick's remarkable play. Finally, the Packers found an answer, stopping Vick on the pivotal fourth and 1 at the Green Bay 42.

Vick was the NFL's national story of the day, throwing for 175 yards and a touchdown and rushing for another 103 yards. He was back and the Eagles apparently had a quarterback controversy.

But Green Bay won the game despite a poor effort

Tramon Williams leaps to intercept a Kevin Kolb pass but receiver DeSean Jackson was able to break up the play. The playmaking Williams enjoyed a breakout season in his first year as a full-time starting cornerback.

from quarterback Aaron Rodgers, who completed just 19 of 31 passes for 188 yards with two touchdowns and two interceptions.

"I played terrible," a disgusted Rodgers said afterward. "It was as bad as I can play. I missed a lot of throws. I personally made too many dumb mistakes."

But some early trends were starting to develop for the Packers. Matthews, whose rookie season the year before had been disrupted by various injuries, proved to be a terror coming off the edge of defensive coordinator Dom Capers' 3-4 defense. He finished with a team-high seven tackles, three quarterback sacks, and a forced fumble. It was obvious the Packers had perhaps their most dynamic and versatile defensive presence since safety Leroy Butler nearly a decade earlier.

Of major concern, though, was the loss in the second quarter of starting tailback Ryan Grant with what at the time was considered a simple sprained ankle. The Packers' perennial 1,000-yard rusher would later be diagnosed with ligament damage in the ankle that would end his season almost before it had begun. It would set a disturbing trend for the Packers.

Still, they had beaten a quality opponent on the road.

Coach Mike McCarthy had seen his defense rise to the occasion and it was a pleasant sight—especially after watching essentially that same defense dramatically collapse during key games the season before.

The defense surrendered 320 total yards and most of that came in the second half when it was still trying to figure out how to stop Vick. Offensively, the Packers churned out 299 yards but McCarthy was not concerned about his offense—it would make plenty of plays.

"It was a gutty performance by our team," McCarthy said. "We are fortunate and pleased to win."

After only one game, the Packers already found themselves with major questions they needed to answer. If Grant was hurt that badly, who would replace him? How could they compete in the tough NFC North with just the rumor of a running game? Was Rodgers' subpar performance an indication of bigger issues or just a slow start?

All those questions, and many others, would all be answered soon enough. The journey had begun. ■

Aaron Rodgers trots off the field with his two favorite targets. Greg Jennings (85) led the Packers in the opener with five catches for 82 yards and a touchdown. Donald Driver (80) contributed five catches and a touchdown of his own.

Paying the Bills

September 19, 2010 • Lambeau Field, Green Bay, Wisconsin

The news was official and awful. The day after the Packers victory over the Eagles, running back Ryan Grant had maintained his ankle injury wasn't all that serious. Medical science said otherwise.

Grant was diagnosed with torn ligaments in his ankle and the Packers didn't even bother wasting any time or energy: they placed him on the injured reserve list September 14 and his season was over after one half, eight carries, and 45 yards.

It was a devastating blow.

Never a great running team in the best of times, the Packers at least had a quality back in Grant who had churned out two straight 1,000-yard seasons since coming to the Packers from the New York Giants in 2007.

He was never widely hailed throughout the league as a great running back, but he had done a solid job in Green Bay, entering the 2010 season with 3,412 rushing yards and coming off a superb 2009 campaign where he gained 1,253 yards and scored 11 touchdowns.

Now Mike McCarthy and the Packers had to fill the void. But how? And with who?

More bad news on the injury front hit the same day when Green Bay placed former first-round draft pick and perennial disappointing defensive tackle Justin Harrell on IR with a knee injury suffered against the Eagles.

Harrell's was a tough story, because he had fought back hard from chronic back issues to finally work his way into the defensive line rotation. He was in shape, he was

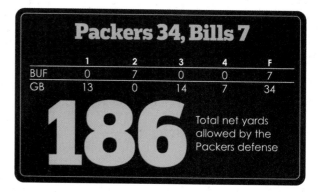

Packers 34, Bills 7

	1	2	3	4	F
BUF	0	7	0	0	7
GB	13	0	14	7	34

186
Total net yards allowed by the Packers defense

playing well, and he seemed ready to finally live up to the potential everyone had seen in him for three years.

"I feel bad for Justin," McCarthy said simply.

But this is the NFL and there is little room for pity. When one guy goes down, another takes his place; that is the way of things.

The Packers had answers for Harrell's loss but not for Grant. And McCarthy admitted as much that week, falling back to the "running back by committee" mantra until something more concrete came along.

Fortunately, the Packers opened their home season against a Buffalo Bills squad that some thought might not win a game all season. As it turned out, the Bulls played tough, hard-nosed football most of the season and never gave up. They proved a tough opponent most weeks but, fortunately, not for the Packers on this September afternoon.

It was a familiar sight for Trent Edwards in Week 2: Clay Matthews closing in for a sack. On this play, Matthews took Edwards down the first of three times. The Green Bay defense also pressured the Buffalo quarterback into throwing three interceptions.

Bolstered by a wonderful defensive effort—again led by Clay Matthews—and a workmanlike offensive performance, the Packers were as good as they needed to be in beating the Bills, 34–7.

Aaron Rodgers played better than he did against the Eagles, completing 19 of 29 passes for 255 yards and throwing touchdown passes to Donald Driver and James Jordan. Rodgers also rushed for 20 yards and scored a touchdown, even attempting a feeble "Lambeau Leap" at the end that drew the good-natured ribbing of his teammates.

"I told them, 'Look I was tired,'" Rodgers cracked afterward.

But despite the rout, the first cracks showed in the dysfunctional running game. The Packers managed just 91 yards on the ground against a poor Bills defense. Brandon Jackson, charged with stepping in for Grant, gained just 26 yards on 11 carries while John Kuhn, a journeyman fullback thrown into the halfback role, led the way with 36 yards.

McCarthy called the running "OK" but he knew better. The Packers weren't going far with a running game like that.

But they would flourish with this defense. Green Bay limited the Bills to 186 total yards, forcing two interceptions and posting four sacks on frazzled Bills' quarterback Trent Edwards. Matthews had five tackles and three more sacks—giving him six for the young season and already staking himself as the early favorite for NFL Defensive Player of the Year.

What made Matthews' early performance so amazing is that he had missed most of training camp with a nagging hamstring injury. Yet when the season began he stepped in without missing a beat.

"I'm just glad he's on our team," Rodgers said.

The Packers had beaten a team they were expected to beat and they had done it at less than full strength. It was a good early sign, but a better test would come the following Monday when they faced their ancient rival the Chicago Bears at Soldier Field. ■

(above) Legendary quarterback Bart Starr is introduced at halftime of the Packers-Bills game. (opposite) Clay Matthews celebrates after dropping Buffalo quarterback Trent Edwards to the turf, in the process becoming the first Packer to record back-to-back three-sack games.

Flag Football

September 27, 2010 • Soldier Field, Chicago, Illinois

It was the great sleeping beast, the elephant in the room that the Green Bay Packers knew they eventually had to confront: for the past three seasons, the Packers had the dubious distinction of being one of the NFL's most penalized teams.

Only the Oakland Raiders, renowned as the NFL's most undisciplined team, was consistently flagged more than the Packers in recent seasons, and Mike McCarthy's frustration was palpable. He preached accountability, and he preached intelligence. He'd plead with his team to read the rule book, for crying out loud. He did what every other team in the NFL did—bring a league referee to training camp to talk about the rules—and he'd have game officials watch practices and call penalties.

Nothing seemed to work and yet, somehow the Packers often overcame penalties by sheer ability and, yes, luck.

But on a key early season Monday night matchup in Chicago those demons finally came home to roost for the frustrated, embarrassed Packers. Ultimately, Green Bay lost to the unbeaten Bears when Robbie Gould kicked a 19-yard field goal with four seconds left in the game. But the seeds for that loss were sown much earlier in the contest.

The Packers were called for a staggering team-record 18 penalties for 152 yards and they were penalties of all sorts—from offsides to personal fouls to pass interference—that kept Bears' drives alive. It was, in short, a complete breakdown of a sort few in the NFL could remember seeing previously. And while the Packers vigorously disputed a

Bears 20, Packers 17

	1	2	3	4	F
GB	7	3	0	7	17
CHI	0	7	0	13	20

152 Total net yards the Packers gave up in committing 18 penalties

number of the penalties, facts were facts, and those penalties went a long way toward the Packers losing their first game of the season.

What made it even more frustrating for the Packers was the fact that despite the lack of discipline, they still outplayed the Bears in nearly every category. Green Bay's offense outgained Chicago 379–276. The Packers kept the ball for more than 35 minutes. The Packers defense held the Bears running game to just 77 yards and allowed just three of nine third-down conversions.

But the Packers also committed two crushing turnovers and allowed Bears return magician Devin Hester to run back a punt 62 yards for a touchdown early in the fourth quarter that changed momentum.

And yet, with all that was seemingly going against the Packers, they still took a 17–14 lead with 6:52 to play on

Aaron Rodgers searches for a running back as Brian Urlacher attacks from his linebacker position. The Bears stymied Green Bay's running game, limiting the Packers to just 63 rushing yards.

Rodgers' 3-yard touchdown run.

Then came the final collapse.

On the Bears' next series, linebacker Frank Zombo was flagged for a 15-yard roughing the passer penalty. Later in the drive, safety Nick Collins was called for unnecessary roughness, another 15 yards. That eventually led to Gould's 25-yard game-tying field goal with 3:59 to play.

Shortly after that, Packers wide receiver James Jones fumbled at the Green Bay 46 and a pass-interference penalty on Green Bay rookie safety Morgan Burnett set up the game-winning field goal.

"We didn't play our best, and we still won," Bears coach Lovie Smith said with a straight face after the game. "That has to mean something."

McCarthy was barely able to control his rage afterward. Whether it was directed at his players, referee Terry McAulay, or a combination was hard to say.

"Can't win that way," he said, tight-lipped.

Still, there were bright spots.

Rodgers played his best all-around game of the young season, completing 34 of 45 passes for 316 yards, his first 300-yard passing game of the campaign. He also directed the Packers on a slick 12-play, 72-yard drive in the fourth quarter for a touchdown that, by all rights, should have been the game-winner.

The Packers also saw what their new weapon at tight end, Jermichael Finley, was capable of accomplishing. Taken in the third round of the 2008 NFL draft out of the University of Texas, Finley was barely 21 years old and at 6-foot-5, 250 pounds the Packers envisioned him as an offensive force—eventually.

After some growing pains and injuries slowed him down, Finley headed into the 2010 season as a matchup nightmare for rival defenses and a featured player in the Packers offense. Against the Bears, he caught nine passes for 115 yards, big numbers for a tight end and just the beginning of what the Packers felt he could do.

But McCarthy was in no mood to celebrate what he had seen. The Packers had big issues to iron out and very little time to do it. ■

John Kuhn rumbles into the Chicago secondary. Mistakes doomed the Packers on this day, with their team-record 18 penalties costing them in a close encounter.

Lion in Wait

October 3, 2010 • Lambeau Field, Green Bay, Wisconsin

Three weeks into the 2010 season, the Green Bay Packers were 2–1 but had yet to put together any kind of performance that would separate them from the rest of the NFC. And so, in hushed tones in some corners and out loud in others, the questions were being asked as to whether the Packers really had what it took to be a contender.

On a gorgeous fall afternoon at Lambeau Field, the Packers could have gone a long way toward providing at least a few answers against the winless, but improving, Detroit Lions.

Everything was on the Packers' side, including a remarkable streak in which the Packers had not lost to the Lions in Wisconsin since 1992—a span of 19 games. But when the game was over, the questions continued to swirl.

"Mike [McCarthy] had to remind us twice in the locker room that we did get a win," fullback John Kuhn said after the game.

Indeed, the Packers seemed well in control of the contest early in the third quarter when cornerback Charles Woodson did what he's always done best—intercepting a Shaun Hill pass 36 seconds into the second half and returning it 48 yards for a touchdown and a 28–14 Packers' lead. But that would be it for the Packers on the scoreboard.

A stiffening Lions defense and a sputtering Packers offense allowed Detroit to battle its way back into the game and make it a lot tighter than it had any right to be.

Packers 28, Lions 26

	1	2	3	4	F
DET	0	14	6	6	26
GB	7	14	7	0	28

22:23 The Packers time of possession against the Lions

After Woodson's interception, the Packers went into hibernation offensively and it wasn't helped by the fact that Aaron Rodgers threw two costly interceptions.

Meanwhile the Lions, behind backup quarterback Shaun Hill, moved the ball at will on the Packers defense. But when they should have scored touchdowns, they could only manage field goals and that was the difference.

Veteran kicker Jason Hanson, who has had his share of success against the Packers over the years, drilled kicks of 39, 52, 49, and 24 yards in the second half to close the gap to two points. Yet, when the Packers offense needed to hang onto the ball the most, they finally managed to do so. And they did it the way no one really expected—by running it.

Holding onto to the slim lead and watching the young Lions growing in confidence on both sides of the

Sandwiched between a pair of Detroit tacklers, Jordy Nelson tries to break free for extra yards. Nelson had a tough day handling return duties, losing a pair of fumbles along the way.

ball, the Packers took over on their own 13-yard line with 6:32 to play. From there, the Packers proceeded to run 12 plays, 10 of them on the ground and featuring—of all people—the burly, largely unknown fullback Kuhn.

Green Bay never had to deal with a third down on the drive and with 55 seconds to play and facing a third down and 7 from the Lions 22, Kuhn ran for eight yards, allowing the Packers to finally breathe a sigh of relief. Kuhn was never expected to be a featured back but McCarthy was learning to work with what he had on the roster. As a result, on that final drive Kuhn carried seven times for 34 yards.

In truth, the Lions outplayed the Packers, gaining 431 yards to Green Bay's 261 yards. Rodgers continued his erratic play, completing just 12 of 17 passes for 181 yards and three touchdowns. But he also threw those two second-half interceptions that kept the Lions alive.

On the positive side, after committing 18 penalties the previous week against the Bears, Green Bay was called for just three penalties against the Lions. But despite a 3–1 record, no one was really happy.

"Doesn't feel like it, does it?" McCarthy said after the game when asked about the team's record.

Rodgers echoed that sentiment. "It's a win, so we're happy about that," he said. "Offensively, we've got to find our identity again."

But the veteran Woodson was left to put it in perspective. "It doesn't matter if it's a good-looking game, an ugly game, it doesn't matter" he said. "As long as you win, that's the main point." ■

(above) Few other teams have as close a bond as the Packers and their Cheesehead fans. (opposite) Jermichael Finley takes the Lambeau Leap after a nine-yard touchdown catch against the Lions—his only score of the season before falling victim to injury.

Mike McCarthy

Coaching Lessons Well-Learned

It was 1999 and Mike McCarthy saw firsthand and way too up close and personal what it was like to be a head coach in the NFL's smallest city. Back then he was still building his resume and learning the ropes of the professional game as the Packers' new quarterbacks coach under first-year head coach Ray Rhodes.

Rhodes had the nearly impossible job of following Mike Holmgren as the Packers' top guy. He had been hand-picked by general Ron Wolf to instill a toughness in the Packers Wolf thought was starting to slip away in Holmgren's final season.

In turn, Rhodes hired a staff of tough guys, including McCarthy, who grew up on the tough streets of Pittsburgh and took no guff from anyone. He was the son of a Pittsburgh cop/bar owner and so he spoke his mind, he said what he meant, and he meant what he said.

McCarthy's job was not necessarily to coach Brett Favre, who was now entering the autumn of his already incredible career, but to make sure Favre kept doing what he did best.

Favre and McCarthy developed a good rapport but the same could not be said of Rhodes and his relationship with Wolf, his players, or the legion of grumbling Packers fans. Rhodes never understood what it took to be a head coach in Green Bay. His gruff, confrontational, angry demeanor was 180 degrees from the affable, approachable

Holmgren. And yet Rhodes might still have survived if he'd won enough.

The 1999 Packers finished 8–8 and were only eliminated from the playoffs on the final day of the season, but a number of coaching blunders, coupled with Wolf's observation that Rhodes had lost control of his team by midseason, forced the GM to do the unthinkable: he fired Rhodes and his entire staff. Even today, Wolf maintains he would have fired Rhodes if the Packers had made the playoffs.

McCarthy saw what had happened and vowed that if he ever became a head coach, he would use his year in Green Bay as a valuable lesson.

For the next six years he learned his craft well, serving as offensive coordinator for both the New Orleans Saints (five seasons) and the San Francisco 49ers (one season) before he interviewed with Packers GM Ted Thompson for the vacant Packers job in January 2006.

He knew the interview had gone well but he also felt Saints offensive coordinator Sean Payton had the inside track for the job. Instead, Thompson called McCarthy three days later and offered him the job.

"It was a dream come true," he said at the time.

But was it really? McCarthy knew only too well what happened to new coaches in Green Bay when they came in unprepared. He remembered the lessons learned back in

A beaming Mike McCarthy speaks at the press conference that announced him as Mike Sherman's successor. He brought with him offensive coordinator experience with both San Francisco and New Orleans.

1999. As a result, McCarthy brought a lunch-bucket familiarity to Green Bay that the Packers embraced immediately.

Whether McCarthy had the other skills necessary to do the job, no one was certain. But his respect for Packers tradition and his self-effacing personality were enough that people wanted to give him every chance to succeed.

Eventually, he proved that he had an innate skill of working with quarterbacks. Favre liked having his old coach back and they resumed a relationship that saw the Packers reach the NFC title game in 2008.

But relationships change. In the spring of 2008, Favre announced his retirement and then changed his mind a few months later. Both McCarthy and Thompson had committed the team's future to Favre's protégé, Aaron Rodgers, angering Favre as well as many Packers fans.

And initially it appeared the critics were right when, despite a 4,000-yard passing season from Rodgers, the Packers stumbled to a 6–10 season. But that was just a hiccup as the Packers rebounded in 2009 with an 11–5 mark and a berth in the playoffs.

McCarthy clearly saved his best work for his fifth season as Packers head coach. At full strength, he knew he had a team that could compete for a Super Bowl. The trouble was, he never had a team at full strength the entire season. He cobbled together bits and pieces of personnel; he found players to fill roles; he changed the offense; he changed the defense; and he instilled in his players the belief that no matter who was on the field, they would succeed.

There would be no excuses. Ever.

In the end, it was a masterful coaching job as Green Bay grabbed a wild-card playoff berth then won three straight postseason games on the road to reach the Super Bowl.

Typically, McCarthy deflected any credit. "It's a tribute to the players," he explained.

But they also had a little help. ■

One of the brightest offensive minds in the NFL, Mike McCarthy has a scheme to maximize the potential of any personnel he puts on the field.

Ambush in D.C.

October 10, 2010 • FedEx Field, Landover, Maryland

In the course of every NFL season, there are dozens, perhaps hundreds, of turning points. There are highs and lows that players, coaches, and fans may not even realize until long after the fact.

There are other times, however, when everyone can recognize rock-bottom when it's staring you in the face. For the 2010 Green Bay Packers, that moment may well have presented itself at FedEx Field on the outskirts of Washington, D.C.

Against an inferior opponent that was already playing poorly, the Packers played down to the level of their competition and found themselves on the short end of a game that they knew very likely could come back and haunt them before the season was over.

There was no reason for the Packers to lose to a Redskins team still seeking an identity after a major roster overhaul brought on by new head coach Mike Shanahan. But the Redskins also faced the Packers at the perfect time—Green Bay was 3–1 but perhaps the most puzzling and puzzled 3–1 team in the NFL.

Little had gone right in the season for the Packers to that point. The offense, which was supposed to be close to unstoppable, was sputtering like an old Chevette. It was even to the point that the Packers sublime stable of receivers were beginning to gripe that they weren't seeing the ball enough.

The defense was playing better but it was not forcing turnovers and it had just been shredded the week before

Redskins 16, Packers 13

	1	2	3	4	OT	F
GB	7	3	3	0	0	13
WSH	0	3	0	10	3	16

427 Total net yards gained by the Packers offense

by a Detroit Lions backup quarterback.

So if the Packers were going to right their ship, this seemed like a perfect place to do it. Instead, as they had done much of the season to date, they struggled early, allowed a bad team to stick around and believe in itself, and then had no answer at the end. Worse, the injury plague that was already hovering over the team, came crashing down with a vengeance.

The ominous portents began on the game's second play when tight end Donald Lee fumbled to the Redskins. In an effort to make a tackle on the play, fellow tight end Jermichael Finley injured his knee and was lost for the game.

But on Green Bay's next series, thanks to a 71-yard run by Brandon Jackson, the Packers scored a touchdown on a Rodgers-to-Lee 5-yard pass.

Washington's Graham Gano kicks the game-winning field goal in overtime, resulting in the first of two consecutive losses in the extra frame for the Packers

A Mason Crosby field goal upped Green Bay's lead to 10–0 but the Packers could not shake the Redskins. It didn't help when the Packers reached the Washington 1 in the second quarter but were stuffed on four downs and could not score

In the second half, the Packers built their tenuous lead to 13–3 before Washington began its comeback. Donovan McNabb hit Anthony Armstrong for a 48-yard touchdown and then with 1:11 left in regulation, Graham Gano kicked a 45-yard field goal to tie the game.

But the Packers had a chance to come back and win in regulation as Rodgers drove them into Redskins territory thanks to two big completions to Green Bay's No. 3 tight end, rookie Andrew Quarless. But with just seven seconds left, Crosby's 53-yard field goal effort strayed left and smacked the left upright—no good.

It only got worse for the Packers in overtime. Deep in their own territory, Rodgers, who had been harassed all day by the Redskins defensive line, was hit hard and threw an interception to LaRon Landry. Not only did the interception set up Gano's game-winning 33-yard field goal, Rodgers suffered a concussion, making his status for the next game uncertain.

Green Bay fell to 3–2 and looked at a growing list of injuries that included their starting quarterback, two tight ends (Finley and Lee), their top defensive player (Clay Matthews), nose guard Ryan Pickett, and safety Derrick Martin.

The Packers piled up 427 total yards, including 115 on the ground by Jackson. Rodgers threw for 293 yards but still didn't look comfortable.

After the game Finley was convinced his injury wasn't serious and figured he'd be out just a week or two. "I still think we can be the team that we want to be," he said.

The trouble was, no one knew what that team was supposed to be. ■

Stretching for extra yards while being tackled by Washington's LaRon Landry, James Jones briefly takes flight. Landry redeemed himself late in the game by setting up the game-winning score with a diving interception.

Hook, Line, and Sinker

October 17, 2010 • Lambeau Field, Green Bay, Wisconsin

It was a week of uncertainty and anxiety for the Green Bay Packers. They had inexplicably lost a game they should have won the week before in Washington but, worse, they had lost a veritable battalion of players—including quarterback Aaron Rodgers who had suffered a concussion on the game's last play.

Given the NFL's newly mandated policy toward head injuries, Rodgers had to go through a stringent battery of tests to prove he was in good enough shape mentally to play the following week against Miami.

There were questions about other players as well—including playmaking tight end Jermichael Finley, who a few days earlier had confidently said his knee injury suffered against Washington was nothing major. Now, unsettling stories were coming out of Green Bay that the injury was a lot more serious than first thought. He would certainly not play against the Dolphins and anything after that was up in the air.

As a team, the Packers were reeling. They had lost twice on last-second field goals but had played so poorly in both games that very little consolation could be taken from how close they were. Indeed, they had played almost as poorly in their three wins. They finally got some good news late in the week when Rodgers was cleared to play. A

Dolphins 23, Packers 20

	1	2	3	4	OT	F
MIA	7	3	3	7	3	23
GB	10	0	0	10	0	20

133 Total receiving yards for Greg Jennings, which included an 86-yard touchdown

home game against an up-and-down Dolphins team seemed like terrific medicine for the Packers.

But a familiar script was about to be written.

A friendly Lambeau Field crowd awaited but the Packers still looked as though they were playing in mud. Despite a scintillating 86-yard touchdown pass from Rodgers to Greg Jennings late in the first quarter, the Dolphins forged a 10–10 halftime tie and led 13–10 after three quarters.

A Mason Crosby field goal tied the game early in the fourth quarter but barely five minutes later Miami reclaimed a 20–13 advantage on a Chad Henne-to-

Aaron Rodgers gets sacked deep in his own territory by the Miami defense. He shook off the effects of a concussion suffered the previous week to throw for 313 yards and a touchdown.

52

Anthony Fasano 22-yard touchdown pass.

Then came what should have been a signature, reputation-defining drive by Rodgers. Despite another physical beating that saw him sacked five times, Rodgers drove the Packers from his own 31 to the Miami 1. Along the way, Rodgers converted a third-and-10 by hitting Jordy Nelson for 24 yards. He also converted a fourth-and-seven by completing a 20-yard pass to Jennings.

Then, on fourth and goal from the 1 with 13 seconds remaining in regulation, Rodgers snuck in for the game-tying touchdown. It was a spectacular, pressure-packed drive and Rodgers had run it flawlessly. But that momentum didn't carry into overtime.

Green Bay did nothing with its lone possession in OT and after a poor punt by Tim Masthay, the Dolphins had to drive only from their 48 to the Green Bay 26 where Dan Carpenter kicked the game-winning field goal.

Three losses and all on last-play field goals. To some, that would look like a team on the verge of being good. To the Packers, and those following, it looked like a team that didn't know how to win. Worse, it looked like a team that lacked heart.

Mike McCarthy was beginning to think it, too, even if he didn't come out and say so. "They've all been tight games," he said in the postmortem. "They've all come down to a critical point in the football game and we're not getting it done at that particular point."

The question was, "Why not?"

Rodgers soldiered through the tough game, completing 18 of 33 passes for 313 yards with a touchdown and an interception. But defensively, the Packers stumbled. With the injured Matthews out of the game, Green Bay surrendered 381 yards to the Dolphins, and wide receiver Brandon Marshall torched the Green Bay secondary for 10 catches and 127 yards.

And, for the first time, Packers players started talking aloud about the damage the injuries were doing to their team. "We need to get some guys back," Rodgers said.

At 3–3, the Packers could not have looked any less like a Super Bowl contender. And waiting in the wings was an old friend. ■

The Miami bench thinks that he stepped out, but Donald Driver continues to sprint down the sideline while stiff-arming Dolphin defenders. Driver caught three passes for 31 yards for Green Bay, who lost despite a sterling effort from their passing game.

Welcome Home

October 24, 2010 • Lambeau Field, Green Bay, Wisconsin

After back-to-back three-point losses and an expanding injury list that would have been comical if it wasn't so serious, the Packers knew they had no margin for error. They were not even halfway through the season and already they were in danger of complete and total irrelevancy when it came to the NFC playoff picture.

And striding into town was the Ghost of Christmas Past, one Brett Lorenzo Favre, and the memories of what he'd done to his former team the year before. During perhaps the best season of his Hall of Fame career, Favre ripped the Packers twice in 2009, throwing for more than 700 yards and seven touchdowns while nearly getting the Vikings into the Super Bowl.

But this was 2010 and Favre's—and the Vikings'—fortunes had dramatically changed. Another solid pick to reach the Super Bowl, the Vikings were struggling even worse than the Packers at 2–3. There were questions on defense, questions about head coach Brad Childress, and Favre had reverted to form, throwing too many interceptions.

In a must-win game for both teams, the Packers finally found their stride. Green Bay's 28–24 victory propelled the Packers forward and sent the Vikings into what amounted to a season-long tailspin. The Packers intercepted Favre three times in the second half and shut down a final, last-minute drive to preserve the win.

"A little payback is nice," said Packers' linebacker Desmond Bishop, who returned one of those interceptions

Packers 28, Vikings 24

	1	2	3	4	F
MIN	7	10	7	0	24
GB	7	7	14	0	28

3 Number of interceptions by Brett Favre in what may have been his last game at Lambeau Field

for a huge touchdown in the third quarter.

In truth, it was a terrific game between two well-matched foes playing for their lives. Aaron Rodgers threw two touchdown passes and Bishop's 32-yard interception return gave the Packers a 28–17 lead. But Favre led the Vikings back, throwing a scoring pass to Randy Moss to cut the margin to 28–24 with an entire quarter to play.

At that point, the Packers defense rose up, as Nick Collins intercepted Favre to end one drive and then at the end of a 17-play drive that reached the Packers 20, Favre's fourth-down pass to Percy Harvin fell incomplete.

The demon was exorcised and, for at least the time being, the Packer season was saved.

Rodgers played a controlled, solid game, rebounding from two bad first-half interceptions to complete 21 of 34 passes for 295 yards and two touchdowns. Favre was

One of the toughest pass-rushers in the league, Jared Allen, breaks through the Green Bay line and gets in the face of Aaron Rodgers. Despite feeling pressure all day, Rodgers threw for 295 yards and a pair of touchdowns.

16-of-29 for 212 yards with one score and three costly picks.

Afterward, embattled Vikings' coach Brad Childress laid much of the blame for the loss at the feet of his quarterback. "Sometimes it's OK to punt the football," Childress said tersely. "You can't give them seven points going the other way."

The attack was stunning and left Favre all but speechless, an unusual state for him. "It's devastating," said Favre, who suffered a sprained ankle being sacked in the fourth quarter. "I take a lot of pride and ownership in all phases of the game and I want the ball in my hands."

It was an impressive, and significant, turnaround for the Packers who finally found a way to win a close game they might not have won even a week earlier. The Packers played smart and with the kind of aggressiveness they hadn't shown in weeks.

Offensively, the Packers spread the ball around and the running game produced just enough to keep the Vikings honest.

It may well have been this game that signaled the Packers' season turnaround. In just the first two weeks of October, the Packers sent to the injured reserve list their best tight end (Finley), a veteran linebacker (Nick Barnett), a promising rookie safety (Morgan Burnett), and a key special teams contributor (Derrick Martin). At that stage, the Packers began to draw together as a unit and decided it would be them against the rest of the world, injuries or not.

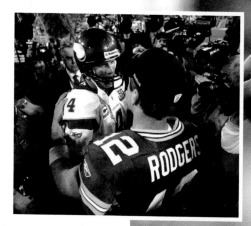

While the Vikings had their own issues to deal with, for the first time all season the Packers began to feel better about who they were and where they were going. The key would be to continue that surge, but the next task was a huge one—facing the high-powered and dangerous New York Jets on the road.

Indeed, just as the Packers began to pull together, they were heading into the nastiest part of their schedule. ■

(above) Two generations of Packers quarterbacks meet at midfield after the game. (opposite) Brett Favre tries, but cannot escape the grasp of linebacker Clay Matthews. Under pressure all game, Favre threw three costly interceptions

Grounded Jets

October 31, 2010 • New Meadowlands Stadium, East Rutherford, New Jersey

It had taken the Green Bay Packers the better part of half a season to figure just who they were and what they needed to do to reach their goals. The process had required a lot of trial and error, a lot of uncertainty, a lot of skill, and more than a little luck.

But after a gutty, tense, crucial win over the Minnesota Vikings the previous week, the Packers were convinced they had turned a corner. They made the plays they needed to make, they executed at the right times, they had found ways to persevere when it seemed like they might.

It was a good start on the road back. But it was only a start.

Now things got really interesting. Over the course of the next several weeks, they'd face the meat of their schedule—playing the AFC power New York Jets, the always-dangerous Dallas Cowboys, the Vikings in the Metrodome, the surging Atlanta Falcons, the improving San Francisco 49ers, the unpredictable Lions at Ford Field, and then a Sunday night clash in Foxboro, Massachusetts, against the always-dynamic New England Patriots.

But it started against the Jets. Those Jets.

Cocky and loud and more than a little obnoxious, by force of will the Jets had made themselves impossible to ignore. They had assembled a formidable football team, adding the likes of running back LaDainian Tomlinson, wide receive Santonio Holmes, and linebacker Jason Taylor to a roster that had reached the AFC title game the year before.

Packers 9, Jets 0

	1	2	3	4	F
GB	3	0	0	6	9
NYJ	0	0	0	0	0

237 Total net yards of offense generated by the Packers

They were 5–1, coming off a bye week and playing at home in front of those hard-to-ignore Jets fans. On the surface, it looked like a nearly impossible task for the Packers.

But these Packers were not the Packers of three weeks earlier. These new Packers, especially on defense, were playing with a swagger of their own, and they bristled at the fact that no one gave them a chance against the AFC power.

The result was an ugly, ragged, miserable fistfight of a football game, but the Packers came out on top, adding another layer to the growing confidence that would propel this team as the season continued.

"We wanted to come in here and prove what we were all about," said linebacker Clay Matthews, who posted a huge fourth quarter sack on quarterback Mark Sanchez "We've had a few close losses that we thought we should have won so we wanted to let our play do our talking."

Mason Crosby raises his arms in celebration after kicking his third field goal of the day. New York cornerback Antonio Cromartie can only watch as the ball sails through the uprights.

The Packers were efficient enough on offense, managing just 237 total yards. But the key was they did not turn the ball over while forcing three Jets turnovers.

The Jets didn't do much to help their own cause, calling a bizarre fake punt in the first half that resulted in a Mason Crosby field goal. They also dropped five passes, suffered two interceptions, and lost a fumble.

"We were a little rusty," coach Rex Ryan said.

Crosby's first field goal staked the Packers to a 3–0 halftime lead. His second field goal came midway through the fourth quarter and was courtesy of a questionable Charles Woodson interception that Jets players were adamant was not.

"Don't get me started on the officiating," Taylor said. "Unless you want to pay my fine."

Nonetheless, Rodgers drove the Packers deep into Jets territory after that takeaway, holding the ball for more than four minutes, and Crosby closed it out with a 21-yard field goal.

The suddenly desperate Jets knew they needed a touchdown, forcing them to try and convert a fourth down deep in their territory with more than two minutes to play. It failed, and the Packers converted a third field goal to secure the unexpected and highly satisfying victory. It was the first Packers road shutout since 1991 and the first time the Jets had been blanked since 2006.

"I wish we could play it again, do it over," an annoyed Ryan said after the game. "But there are no do-overs in this league."

It was yet another step in the right direction for the Packers who could palpably feel their fortunes changing. "We wanted to come in here and match the Jets' intensity and show them we can play with anybody," safety Nick Collins said afterward.

Mission accomplished. ◼

Unfazed by the windy conditions, Greg Jennings hauled in six catches for 81 yards against the Jets. Mark Sanchez outdueled Aaron Rodgers in the tough weather, but it was the Packers who blanked the home side.

Dallas Destruction

November 7, 2010 • Lambeau Field, Green Bay, Wisconsin

One mark of a good team is how it handles an opponent that is desperate and on the ropes. Does it allow that team to stick around and gain confidence? Or does it further perpetuate that team's misery and never, ever give it a chance to gain hope, much less victory?

A month earlier, the Packers had been the kind of team that nearly ran itself out of the playoff race before it even really had begun. They allowed the likes of the Lions, Redskins, and Dolphins to remain competitive in games in which they had no business being competitive. The result? Two overtime losses and a close win.

Since that time the Packers had learned a few lessons about how to start and finish game. They now knew that once you had a team down, you had to be ruthless and unapologetic. Put the hammer down and move on to the next game. And facing them on a Sunday night national stage at Lambeau Field was the prime example of team spinning out of control—the Dallas Cowboys.

Tabbed as a Super Bowl contender before the season began, Wade Phillips' team was a mess. They had lost five in a row, sat 1–6, and had lost their starting quarterback Tony Romo to a broken collarbone. It was going so badly for the once-proud franchise that rumors were swirling that owner Jerry Jones would fire Phillips if things got much worse.

They were about to get much worse.

In their most complete display of the season, the Packers first outplayed, then overwhelmed, and finally

Packers 45, Cowboys 7

	1	2	3	4	F
DAL	0	7	0	0	7
GB	0	28	7	10	45

28 Number of points the Packers exploded for in the second quarter, which included two passing TDs, one running TD, and one fumble return for a TD

embarrassed the Cowboys. It was Green Bay's third straight win and easily its most complete.

"There's a lot of confidence in that locker room," quarterback Aaron Rodgers said afterward. "We were 3–3 and coming off two straight losses in overtime and there were definitely some doubts creeping in, wondering what the last 10 games would do for us and realizing we had to make a push."

The Packers never gave the Cowboys a chance to breathe, burying them under 28 second-quarter points and making the rest of the game all but irrelevant. The Packers did everything they needed to do: they were dominating on offense and defense, they forced turnovers, and once they had the Cowboys down, they made sure they were soon out.

Two Rodgers' touchdown passes, a Brandon Jackson

Charles Woodson reacts after breaking up a pass. The Green Bay defense turned in one of its most dominant performances of the season, all but sealing the fate of soon-to-be-fired Dallas coach Wade Phillips.

run, and a Nick Collins return of a fumble staked the Packers to a 28–0 lead that they extended to 35–7 after three quarters. In the fourth quarter, Clay Matthews added the final indignity, returning a Jon Kitna interception 62 yards for a touchdown and a 45–7 final scored that left the Cowboys dazed and bewildered.

The Packers piled up 415 total yards to Dallas' 205. The defense forced four turnovers, giving it seven over two games. Meanwhile, Rodgers continued to play superbly, completing 27 of 34 passes for 289 yards and three scores. As well, he had gone two straight games without throwing an interception and was recapturing the form that had made him dangerous the year before.

Even the running game—which had been little more than a suggestion much of the season—was efficient, gaining 139 yards thanks to the trio of Brandon Jackson, John Kuhn, and Rodgers, who had started to run when necessary.

Meanwhile, the Cowboys were lost. "You're going to keep working, you're going to keep moving forward," an ashen Phillips said after the game. "It sounds like a hollow message now, but that's really the way it is."

The dismantling at the hands of the Packers left Jones nearly speechless afterward though he did admit there were so many problems to solve he was running out of fingers on his hand to count them. Two days later, Jones made the only decision he could really make—he fired Phillips and inserted offensive coordinator Jason Garrett as head coach.

Indirectly, perhaps, the Packers had forced another team to make a drastic midseason decision.

The Green Bay Packers were back in the national conversation not only as a playoff team, but a dangerous playoff team—one of those clubs no one wants to face in the postseason.

The Packers wanted to prove the talk was justified, but they would have to wait to do that in two weeks—following a bye—by taking care of business in one of their least favorite places on the planet. ■

Aaron Rodgers lines up behind center Scott Wells. The offensive line, hampered by injuries earlier in the year, turned in its best performance of the season against the hapless Cowboys.

A Good Bye

November 21, 2010 • Hubert H. Humphrey Metrodome, Minneapolis, Minnesota

No team needed a break more than the 2010 Green Bay Packers. It had, quite frankly, been one hell of a season and the most important part still loomed like gathering storm clouds on the horizon.

The roller-coaster began with a 2–0 start. It then degenerated with three losses in four games that had nearly everyone questioning the Packers' skill, tenacity, and heart. The wild ride continued with three straight wins, including a rout of the proud Dallas Cowboys that had forced the midseason firing of their head coach.

And while many teams might have wanted the recent upswing to continue uninterrupted, the Packers were one of the last teams to celebrate their bye week and they welcomed it. Nine straight weeks of football and an unceasing array of injuries had emptied the team's tank. A week off allowed players to heal up and offered the opportunity for the collective team mentality to recharge for what promised to be an engaging stretch run.

The first order of business was a rematch with the Minnesota Vikings in the Metrodome, a place that, more often than not, had been a house of horrors for the Packers. So Green Bay knew they could not take anything for granted–especially against this team, this quarterback, and in this venue.

Still, if the Dallas Cowboys had been on the road to oblivion when Green Bay faced them two weeks earlier, the Vikings were clearly on the same off-ramp. Brett Favre's performances had not improved. The Vikings

Packers 31, Vikings 3

	1	2	3	4	F
GB	0	17	7	7	31
MIN	3	0	0	0	3

4 Number of Aaron Rodgers touchdown passes, including three to Greg Jennings.

were still out of sync and the organization was in turmoil after coach Brad Childress had inexplicably released wide received Randy Moss a week earlier, without telling the players or his boss, owner Zygi Wilf.

So the Vikings appeared to be ripe for beating and after a slow start, the Packers obliged.

Trailing 3–0 after one quarter, the Packers finally got in gear in the second quarter. Mason Crosby's 42-yard field goal with 9:44 left tied the game and on their next possession, the Packers drove 80 yards on eight plays with Rodgers hitting Greg Jennings for the touchdown and a 10–3 lead.

But the Packers weren't done.

Cornerback Tramon Williams intercepted Favre late in the quarter and Rodgers again drove the Packers into scoring position, capping the drive with a three-yard

The Packers defense—here led by Atari Bigby (20) and Frank Zombo—bottled up Adrian Peterson and the Minnesota offense, keeping the Vikings out of the end zone.

scoring toss to James Jones with three seconds remaining.

The Packers kept their foot on the accelerator to start the third quarter as Rodgers connected with Jennings for a 46-yard score and a 24–3 lead that completely sucked the oxygen out of the Metrodome and its crowd.

Rodgers capped his exceptional day with a fourth-quarter scoring pass to Jennings and by that point, the boos were raining down on the home team. "I'm at loss for words," Favre said in his postgame press conference. "Disappointing doesn't begin to say it."

Rodgers was clearly in a groove now. He completed 22 of 31 passes for 301 yards and four touchdowns—three to the electric wideout Jennings. For the third straight game, the Packers did not commit a turnover, but they forced two by the Vikings.

This was the Green Bay Packers team everyone had expected to see weeks earlier. "We're going to be tough to beat when we're playing like that," Rodgers said.

Meanwhile, in an eerie similarity to what had transpired in the Cowboys' game, the Vikings were imploding in front of everyone. Favre, who suddenly looked old and disinterested, was arguing with his offensive coordinator and close friend, Darrell Bevell, on the sideline, and Childress appeared to be a man preparing for a trip to the gallows.

And indeed, two days after being hammered by the Packers, Wilf relieved Childress of his job. In what may be an NFL record, the Packers had now been party to two straight coaches losing their jobs.

Nothing like that figured to happen the following week as the Packers prepared for perhaps the NFC's best team, the Atlanta Falcons. But the Packers were playing with the kind of confidence they hadn't known for a while.

"We've got a foot on the gas, our hands on the wheel, and we're looking straight ahead," coach Mike McCarthy said after the game. ■

Brandon Jackson (32) carries the ball during the first half against the Vikings. Despite the rout, the Packers running game continued to sputter, generating only 91 yards and no touchdowns.

Aaron Rodgers

Proving the Doubters Wrong

Aaron Rodgers will never forget. He swears he doesn't think about it all the time like he once did, but Aaron Rodgers will never forget.

It was April 23, 2005, the first day of the NFL Draft, and what would prove to be the worst—and ultimately the best—day of his life.

Rodgers was sitting just off stage at the New York City draft site awaiting his coronation as a high first-round pick as well as the millions of dollars, accolades, and endorsements that would surely come his way.

Then the draft began. One by one players slipped off the board ahead of him. The first pick? Utah quarterback Alex Smith, selected by Rodgers' hometown team, the San Francisco 49ers. And so it continued. Players like Ronnie Brown, Erasmus James, Derrick Johnson, Travis Johnson, David Pollack, Troy Williamson, Matt Jones.

Matt Jones?

As the room emptied of draft invitees who had been selected and feted with their celebratory introduction, there sat Rodgers—stunned, angry, confused, and humiliated.

The Packers, ready to exercise the 24th pick of the first round, were amazed to find Rodgers' name still on the board. In most cases, NFL teams take their full allotment of 15 minutes in the first round to decide who they want to draft. The Packers wasted no time and, even though they had one of the game's best quarterbacks in Brett Favre, they snapped up Rodgers without hesitation.

It may have been the biggest steal in NFL Draft history. Of the 23 players selected ahead of Rodgers, three are out of football altogether and a number of others, including Smith, are still struggling to make a name for themselves in the league.

Aaron Rodgers proved everyone wrong—again. It has been something he's done very well over the years.

He was not highly recruited out of high school in Chico, California. He had an offer to walk on at the University of Illinois, but he declined and played one season at Butte Community College near his home. The next summer, University of California head coach Jeff Tedford was recruiting Rodgers' BCC teammate, tight end Garrett Cross, and Rodgers offered to throw to him during the workout. Tedford signed Cross but he was surprised and intrigued by Rodgers, whom he signed as well.

Rodgers took over as Cal's starting quarterback for the next two seasons, throwing for 5,500 yards and 43 touchdowns while leading the Bears to two bowl games. Rodgers decided to forego his senior season and go into the draft where he expected to be a top-10 pick at worst.

After that humbling April day in 2005, Rodgers went to Green Bay expecting to learn at the knee of one of the game's great QBs. But the new guy learned quickly what many of Green Bay's former back-up quarterbacks already knew—Favre was not in the teaching business. Rodgers absorbed what he could and, while he and Favre had a

Aaron Rodgers looks to throw downfield after scrambling outside the pocket. He entered Super Bowl XLV as the NFL career leader for postseason passer rating.

good relationship, this was not going to be a warm-and-fuzzy teacher-pupil deal. Rodgers was the heir apparent and Favre had no intention of relinquishing the job easily.

For three years, Rodgers sat and watched and learned what he could until a late 2007 opportunity to show his stuff presented itself. Rodgers relieved an injured Favre during a nationally televised game in Dallas and nearly led the Packers to a win over the favored Cowboys. He looked ready to be a starter.

When the Favre retirement soap opera erupted in 2008, Mike McCarthy and Ted Thompson were quick to anoint Rodgers as their new quarterback. By training camp, when Favre changed his mind and asked for his job back, it was too late: the Packers had moved on. When Favre, the face and soul of the organization was dealt to the New York Jets, Rodgers became, in the eyes of some fans, the bad guy.

All Rodgers did in reply was go about his job. His first season as starter, he threw for 4,000-plus yards and 28 touchdowns and played through a separated shoulder and bad ankle.

The next season, he threw for 4,400 yards with 30 touchdown and just seven interceptions. Despite the gaudy numbers, Rodgers failed in his first opportunity to win a playoff game, in the process fumbling while getting sacked in overtime.

His toughness and tenacity showed through again in 2010. He missed one game with a concussion yet still threw for 3,922 yards, 28 touchdowns, and just 11 interceptions. He also completed nearly 66 percent of his passes. As well, he rushed for 356 yards and four scores and was Green Bay's second-leading rusher.

Rodgers says he doesn't think about April 2005 anymore, and he probably doesn't. But there are surely NFL general managers who are thinking about that day and wondering how their fortunes would be different with Rodgers as their quarterback. ■

Rodgers celebrates after rushing for a nine-yard touchdown against Buffalo. Running is an underrated part of his game—Rodgers' ability to move in the pocket and scramble for big gains is part of what makes the Green Bay offense so deadly.

A Matter of Matts

November 28, 2010 • Georgia Dome, Atlanta, Georgia

Through their four-game winning streak, the Packers had met two teams that were the very definition of dysfunction—the Minnesota Vikings (twice) and the Dallas Cowboys. The third team, the New York Jets, probably didn't take the Packers all that seriously and it cost them.

Such was not going to be case against the Atlanta Falcons, an exciting young team that was playing with as much, if not more, confidence than the Packers. The Falcons featured an unflappable third-year quarterback in Matt Ryan, who had lost only once in the Georgia Dome. At 8–2 and all but assured of a playoff spot, the Falcons were positioning themselves for an NFC South title, the best record in the NFC, and a critical first-round playoff bye.

There was not a whiff of turmoil with Mike Smith's team, and they took the Packers very seriously. The result was a terrific game that offered a glimpse of what might come in the postseason. It was a game that encompassed all that was going well with the Packers in recent weeks. But it also revealed a few nagging issues that kept Green Bay from attaining the elite status it was looking for.

The Falcons grabbed a quick 3–0 lead on a Matt Bryant field goal. But the Packers responded with a nice drive from their own 15 to the Atlanta 4 that ended in a Mason Crosby field goal.

Then came a turning point and the first sign that what had been going so well the previous month might be absent on this day.

Falcons, 20, Packers 17

	1	2	3	4	F
GB	3	0	7	7	17
ATL	3	7	0	10	20

12 Number of rushing attempts by Aaron Rodgers, who led the team in rushing with 51 yards, including a TD

The Packers embarked on a nearly eight-minute drive that started at their 15 and went to the Falcons' 1. Amazingly, the first nine plays of the drive were all passes. On first down and goal from the 2, Rodgers tried to sneak in for the score but was stopped a yard short. On second down, he tried again and this time he fumbled at the goal line.

The ball was recovered by Falcons linebacker Mike Peterson and a chance to take an important lead was gone. It was Green Bay's first turnover in 15 quarters, the team's longest streak since 1963. "That's what lost the game," Rodgers said.

But it wasn't, because the Packers had more opportunities.

The Falcons grabbed a 10–3 halftime lead on Ryan's short touchdown pass to Tony Gonzalez late in the second quarter but Green Bay tied the game again in third quarter

After a big kickoff return by Eric Weems put the Falcons in prime field position, Matt Bryant booted a 47-yard field goal with nine seconds left to give Atlanta the comeback win over Green Bay.

when Rodgers scored from a yard out with 7:17 remaining.

One more time, the Falcons took the lead, this time on Michael Turner's one-yard blast in the first minute of the fourth quarter.

The Packers had a final opportunity when they took over the ball with 5:59 to play. One more time, Rodgers executed a nearly flawless drive despite being harassed constantly by the Falcons defense. He moved the Packers from their own 10 to the Atlanta 10, converting a huge fourth down along the way.

Then, on fourth and goal from the Falcons' 10, Rodgers rolled left, bought time, and then fired a laser into the end zone that connected with Jordy Nelson for the score with 56 seconds left in regulation.

It was an epic drive at the perfect time.

"I was thinking overtime at that point," Rodgers said.

But things didn't quite work out that way. Eric Weems took the kickoff and was tackled by Green Bay's Matt Wilhelm, who grabbed Weems' facemask as he brought him down. The Packers were flagged for the 15-yard penalty, giving the Falcons the ball at the Green Bay 49. Ryan then completed four straight passes to put kicker Matt Bryant in position for the game-winning field goal.

After a Packers timeout, Bryant stepped up and coolly drilled the 47-yarder with nine second remaining.

The loss ended Green Bay's four-game winning streak but offered enough positive clues that they were still on the right track.

Rodgers hit on 26 of 35 passes for 344 yards and one score. For the fourth straight game, he did not throw an interception. But the Packers also reverted to their reckless days, committing eight penalties for 66 yards, the most they'd had since the disaster in Chicago on Week 2.

"It's discouraging not winning a game we should have won," Rodgers said. ∎

James Jones powers through a pair of Falcons defensive backs. Jones had five catches for 44 yards, going into some tough spaces to keep drives alive.

Some Starks Reality

December 5, 2010 • Lambeau Field, Green Bay, Wisconsin

From the moment starting tailback Ryan Grant went down with a season-ending ankle injury in the season-opener against the Philadelphia Eagles, the Packers knew they would, eventually, have to deal with the issue of their crippled running game.

Conventional NFL wisdom has always stated that teams do not advance (or at least advance very far) in the playoffs without some semblance of a rushing attack. Balance is required, if for no other reason than to give an opposing defense something else to think about besides a quarterback dropping back and looking for an open receiver.

For 11 games, the Packers had been getting by with a rushing game bound together with chewing gum and chicken wire.

Brandon Jackson tried but lacked the power and speed to be a true breakaway back. John Kuhn was a fullback, first, last, and always, though he did his best. Indeed, quarterback Aaron Rodgers was probably Green Bay's best option running the ball. He could scramble but, more to the point, he was elusive in the pocket and had slipped away from more tackles than anyone could count. But a running quarterback is also a recipe for disaster.

In 12 games, the Packers best running performance was 157 yards against the Redskins and 71 of that came on one Jackson run. In that same span, the Packers were averaging about 100 yards per game on the ground but for less than the average of the magical

Packers 34, 49ers 16

	1	2	3	4	F
SF	3	10	3	0	16
GB	0	14	14	6	34

37:11 The Packers time of possession in the game

four yards per gain teams seek.

Indeed, too often at the end of games, when a five-yard run might seal a victory, the Packers had to throw to ensure the same result.

It was now December and with crunch time coming, the Packers needed an answer at running back.

In a rugged 34–16 win over the puzzling San Francisco 49ers at Lambeau Field, the Packers appeared to find what they were looking for—and it came from a most unusual place: rookie James Starks, a sixth-round draft pick out of the University of Buffalo. He had missed his entire senior season in college due to a shoulder injury and started his pro career on the Physically Unable to Perform list with a leg injury. But when Starks got the call, he responded.

With 73 yards on 18 carries, the powerful Starks gave the Packers an option they'd been lacking. He was also

After pulling into the open field, Daryn Colledge looks to make a block on a San Francisco defender. The sturdy guard has started nearly every game in his five-season professional career.

complemented by Jackson, Kuhn, and Rodgers. Between the four of them, the Packers rushed for 136 yards, their third-highest total of the season.

"We needed that," said coach Mike McCarthy, who had been waiting all season for Starks to recover from various, nagging injuries. It was a new wrinkle for a Packers team that was becoming more dangerous as the weeks went by.

The Packers only led the 49ers 14–13 at halftime and seemed destined to struggle against another inferior foe. Then, early in the third quarter, came one of the most memorable plays of the Packers season, if not in team history.

Veteran wide receiver Donald Driver, who was slowed by a case of food poisoning suffered the night before, took a short pass from Rodgers and then, through sheer determination and maybe some poor technique by the Niners, broke seven tackles. As 49er defenders continued to climb on him, Driver pushed forward and eventually, 61 yards later, dove into the end zone for the touchdown.

"I don't know what happened," a smiling Driver said later. "All I know is that when I caught it, I just started making moves."

"It was one of the greatest plays I've ever been a part of," Rodgers marveled.

From that stage, the Packers were never really threatened. Rodgers completed 21 of 30 passes for 298 yards and three touchdowns. With Starks running hard, the Packers averaged four yards per rush and that made McCarthy happy.

"They just imposed their will on us," 49ers linebacker Takeo Spikes said. "It was embarrassing."

The Packers were throwing the ball and running it with some authority. The defense was playing superbly and the special teams weren't causing any major problems. Everything seemed in place a major late-season run and, just maybe, a first-round bye in the playoffs.

But one play can change a game and a season. And the Packers were about to learn that lesson the hard way. ■

(above) Green Bay fans are famous for their tailgate spreads. (opposite) The newly healthy James Starks breaks into the San Francisco secondary. He had a fine day, rushing for 73 yards on 18 carries as the Packers pulled away from the 49ers.

A Kick in the Head

December 12, 2010 • Ford Field, Detroit, Michigan

Everyone knew it but no one talked about it. As it had been for all those years with Brett Favre, so it was now with Aaron Rodgers. These Green Bay Packers would go as far as their quarterback would take them, and if he got hurt…well…that thought was too awful to contemplate.

But that couldn't happen—could it? Rodgers, who had been criticized in 2009 for holding the ball too long and absorbing too many sacks, had grown a lot smarter in 2010. He was getting rid of the ball quicker, eluding tacklers better, throwing the ball away when necessary. All was good, right?

There was one thing Rodgers still hadn't learned or at least would not do with any consistency—at the end of a scramble, he needed to give himself up with a feet-first slide. Too often, he'd dive headfirst and take a blow he didn't need to take. Coach Mike McCarthy, a one-time quarterbacks coach, harped on his star to follow the standard procedure but either Rodgers forgot or didn't care for the policy.

Ultimately, Rodgers' hubris caught up with him on the unforgiving artificial surface of Ford Field in Detroit, Michigan.

Under second-year coach Jim Schwartz, the Lions were developing into a pretty good team. Though they had won just twice in 2010, they had played hard every week and were a break or two away becoming a team to truly reckon with. The Packers needed no more evidence

Lions 7, Packers 3

	1	2	3	4	F
GB	0	0	3	0	3
DET	0	0	0	7	7

66 Total net yards rushing for the Packers offense

of this than their first meeting in early October when they escaped with a two-point win.

Now the Lions believed in themselves as a team and knew a win over a top-notch foe would only help catapult them further.

It all played out just as the Lions had hoped.

The Packers were sluggish early on. Tight end Andrew Quarless lost a fumble on Green Bay's second play from scrimmage and later in the quarter, Rodgers threw his first interception in five games.

But the Lions were no better. Down to No. 3 quarterback Drew Stanton after injuries to Matthew Stafford and Shaun Hill, they turned the ball over twice and could mount nothing on offense.

Then, with three minutes left before halftime, Rodgers was flushed from the pocket and took off, running 18 yards

A trio of Detroit defenders stymies Brandon Jackson. It was a tough day on the ground for the Packers running backs; Jackson was the leading runner with just 19 yards on seven carries.

before he was tackled by Amari Spievy and Landon Johnson. Diving forward, as was his habit, Rodgers' head smacked the turf hard and he stayed on the ground for several seconds. After calling a timeout to clear his head, Rodgers was sacked on the next play.

As the third quarter opened, backup Matt Flynn was under center for the Packers, and Rodgers was sidelined with his second concussion of the season.

A seventh-round pick in 2008, Flynn had studied hard under Rodgers for two years. His ability impressed the Packers enough that they jettisoned Brian Brohm, a second-round choice in the same draft. Flynn played okay for being thrust into a tough situation, but he could not generate any offense against an inspired Lions defense.

Detroit finally scored on a short Stanton-to-Will Heller touchdown pass with just under eight minutes to play.

Flynn led the Packers back to the Detroit 31 but on fourth down his pass into the end zone to a diving Greg Jennings fell incomplete. It was the Lions first win over an NFC North foe since October 2007, a span of 19 games and it snapped a 10-game losing streak to the Packers.

It was a devastating loss in more ways than one for the Packers. Afterward, McCarthy said he wasn't sure how badly Rodgers was hurt.

"I really can't measure the level of the concussion at this point," he said. "I was just told that his head is clear and he has a headache."

But the early reports were already suggesting Rodgers would not be ready for the next game and it would fall on the inexperienced Flynn to travel to New England and face the powerful Patriots.

The win was clearly a turning point for the Lions. And the loss was threatening to be a turning point for the Packers, too. ■

The Packers take the turf at Ford Field on a forgettable day. They suffered an upset loss in an ugly game and lost quarterback Aaron Rodgers to his second concussion of the season.

Charles Woodson

Defensive Leader of the Pack

It didn't make the splash that Reggie White's signing did more than a decade earlier. But when perennial All-Pro cornerback Charles Woodson signed with the Green Bay Packers in 2006, a new era for the team began.

When Green Bay won the Reggie White free-agency sweepstakes in 1993, beating out powerhouses like the San Francisco 49ers and Washington Redskins, the Packers signaled they were ready to take their place among the NFL big boys. Three years later, the Packers were in the Super Bowl.

Woodson's arrival in Green Bay was slightly less dramatic, but no less significant. The 1997 Heisman Trophy winner had spent eight seasons with the Oakland Raiders, even earning a spot in Super Bowl XXXVII in 2002, a disastrous 48–21 loss to Tampa Bay that haunted Woodson for years.

After the 2005 season, the Raiders had had enough of Woodson's up-and-down play and frequent antics, and Woodson had had more than enough of a Raiders organization collapsing around him. He signed with the Packers in 2006 but it wasn't as though there were a dozen teams breaking down his door to sign him. He was thought to be at the end of a good career that should have been better. And he came to a Packers team that was suddenly adrift.

In 2005, Green Bay stumbled to a 4–12 season, its worst since 1991, which cost Mike Sherman his job as head coach. The untested Mike McCarthy was the new coach and he was already having to deal with questions as to whether his franchise player—Brett Favre—still wanted to play.

Into this uncertainty stepped Woodson and in five seasons in Green Bay, his transformation has been a revelation. The cocky player known for falling asleep in team meetings in Oakland has evolved into a legitimate team leader in Green Bay. And with each passing season, when time says his skills should be diminishing, they are instead improving.

In 2009 Woodson intercepted nine passes (returning three for touchdowns) and was named the NFL Defensive Player of the Year. In 2010 he may have had an even better all-around season. He recorded 92 tackles, 13 passes defensed, and five forced fumbles. He only intercepted two passes, but he brought one back for a key touchdown against the Lions. His other pick stopped a New York Jets drive.

Amazingly, in eight seasons in Oakland, Woodson had just 17 interceptions. In five seasons with the Packers, he's had 30 and now owns the club record for most defensive returns for a touchdown (eight interceptions and one fumble) that was previously held by Darren Sharper and Herb Adderley.

"I can't imagine being anywhere else now," Woodson has said time and again.

If Woodson has been a godsend for the Packers, the

Charles Woodson has been a star for Green Bay since he arrived as a free agent after the 2005 season, but his impact has been greatest working in Dom Capers' aggressive 3-4 scheme.

Packers have been just as important for Woodson. Under defensive coordinator Dom Capers, he is playing corner-back the way he always wanted to play. He blitzes off the edge; he takes on the other team's wide receiver; and he is allowed to be aggressive and take the chances that come with a team showing complete confidence in his ability.

And he has become the consummate leader—so much so that he was asked to give the team's pregame pep talk prior to the NFC title game against the Bears.

"I think the guys have a lot of respect for me and my career," Woodson told *USA Today.* "You lead by example but at times you're needed to speak. It's something I'm comfortable with, and it has worked so far."

His message before the NFC Championship Game? Playing off the fact that President Obama, a longtime Chicago resident and a Bears fan, said he would attend the Super Bowl if his Bears won, Woodson said simply, "He doesn't want to come see us at the Super Bowl…. Guess what? We're going to see him."

The locker room erupted and the Packers won.

"It was just a spur-of-the-moment thing," Woodson said with a smile.

Perhaps no one appreciates being in a Super Bowl more than Woodson, one of just two Packers to have played in one before. (The other is nose tackle Ryan Pickett, when he played for the St. Louis Rams.)

"The thing is, you never know when you'll get back," Woodson told *USA Today.* "You never know if you'll get there. You never know if you'll win one."

And despite having played 13 seasons, an eternity in the NFL, Woodson has no plans on retiring anytime soon.

"Having too much fun," he said. ∎

Woodson is congratulated by teammates after recovering a fumble against the Eagles. He holds the Packers' record for interceptions in a single season and has been a Pro Bowler each of the last three years.

No Room for Error

December 19, 2010 • Gillette Stadium, Foxborough, Massachusetts

There were no flowery pre-game speeches for this one. Nothing Knute Rockne-esque or Vince Lombardi-like about what the Packers needed to do or what the future held.

This was backs-against-the-wall time for the Green Bay Packers, and they knew it better than anyone. They had to travel to Massachusetts and meet the hottest team in football, the New England Patriots. It would be a tough assignment even with all their pieces in place.

But they would have to play without Aaron Rodgers, their leader and best offensive player. Rodgers suffered a concussion the week before against the Lions and had not passed the NFL-mandated tests required to go back on the field.

So that was that. The Packers would go to war with Matt Flynn, a capable backup with the heart of lion but no meaningful experience. In public, the Packers spoke glowingly of Flynn, a smart guy who had the moxie to lead LSU to a national championship three seasons earlier. Privately, no one really knew how he'd perform on a national stage.

He had done OK in relief duty of Rodgers the week before, completing 15 of 26 passes for 177 yards. But he threw a disastrous interception deep in Lions' territory and could not generate any touchdowns when it mattered.

But that was all ancient history. Flynn would have to produce and he'd need help.

In the end, the Packers lost the game, but in defeat they

Patriots 31, Packers 27

	1	2	3	4	F
GB	3	14	7	3	27
NE	7	7	7	10	31

71

Total yards Patriots' 313-lb. offensive lineman Dan Connolly rumbled for on a kickoff return

may well have saved their season. Indeed, they outplayed the Patriots, they shut down quarterback Tom Brady, they moved the ball on the Patriots defense, and—one more time—they learned something new about themselves.

The Packers did not shrink from the 11–2 Patriots and proceeded to hit them in the mouth every chance they got. In fact, Green Bay opened the game by recovering a surprise onside kick that led to a field goal and a quick 3–0 lead.

Flynn, looking as calm as if he'd been starting all season, threw second-quarter touchdown passes of 1 yard to Greg Jennings and 66 yards to James Jones and Green Bay took a 17–14 halftime lead to the locker room.

Unfortunately for the Packers, that lead would have been bigger if it hadn't been a disastrous special teams' breakdown.

After the TD pass to Jennings made it 17–7 with 2:12

Matt Flynn played well in place of the injured Aaron Rodgers, throwing for 251 yards and his first three NFL touchdowns. Unfortunately, Flynn was sacked on fourth down to end the Packer's desperate last-second drive for a game-winning touchdown.

left in the half, Mason Crosby kicked the ball short to avoid the Patriots dangerous return men. Dan Connolly, a 313-pound lineman, scooped up the ball and the Packers, instead of just tackling the big guy, tried to strip the ball. Connolly rumbled 71 yards to the Packers' 4. Two plays later, Brady connected with Aaron Hernandez for a touchdown.

"We did a poor job of tackling on that," coach Mike McCarthy said in the understatement of the season.

But the Packers continued to hang around in the second half. Another Flynn touchdown, this one of six yards to John Kuhn, in the third quarter and a 19-yard Crosby field goal early in the fourth quarter, staked the Packers to a 27—21 lead.

But the Patriots battled back and, midway through the fourth quarter, took the lead for good on a Brady-to-Hernandez touchdown.

Flynn had one more drive in him and with 4:22 left, moved from his own 43 to the New England 15. But on fourth-and-1, Flynn's inexperience finally caught up with him. The play was late coming in and confusion abounded. Flynn tried to throw but was sacked, ending the game.

Flynn acquitted himself well, completing 24 of 37 passes for 251 yards and three scores. The Packers out-gained the Patriots 369-249 and Brady, the odds-on favorite to win the season MVP, was held to just 163 passing yards.

"Our plan was just to go out there and cut it loose," Flynn said. "The plan didn't change because I was out there; we went out there and went after them. We just didn't get it done."

With the loss, the Packers sat at 8–6 and were in serious danger of missing the playoffs. The division title was gone—secured that same day by the Bears—and now the Packers had to win their final two games to reach the postseason.

It was a daunting task but one of their own making. Now they'd really find out what they were made of. ■

(above) Though he was out-passed by Matt Flynn, Tom Brady showed why he remains one of the league's elite quarterbacks. He threw for 163 yards and two touchdowns, yet again coming through in the clutch. (opposite) Aaron Rodgers takes the field, but had to be content watching in street clothes as he missed the game with a concussion.

Giant Comeback

December 26, 2010 • Lambeau Field, Green Bay, Wisconsin

The math was as simple as it could get. Because of circumstances and injuries and erratic play and bad luck and all the other things that can happen in the course of a season, the 2010 Packers found themselves on the brink of missing the playoffs. Then again, they also found themselves on the brink of making the playoffs.

Their fate would be determined by what happened in the final two games of the season. Simply put, if the Packers beat the New York Giants and the Chicago Bears they would reach the postseason…and then, of course, anything could happen after that.

But stumble—as they did in Chicago or in Washington or at home against the Dolphins or in Detroit—then it was all over and the Packers would likely have the distinction of being one of the most talented teams not to make the playoffs.

"It's all still in front of us," quarterback Matt Flynn said after the loss last week to the Patriots.

Indeed, it was in front of them, and the journey began at Lambeau Field the day after Christmas against a Giants team that was almost as mercurial as the Packers.

The week before the Giants had been in control of their future but inexplicably lost a fourth-quarter lead and ultimately a game to the Eagles. That left them on the precipice of playoff elimination alongside the Packers.

The Packers welcomed back Aaron Rodgers from his concussion and he proceeded to throw first-quarter touchdown passes of 80 yards to Jordy Nelson and three

Packers 45, Giants 17

	1	2	3	4	F
NYG	0	14	3	0	17
GB	14	7	10	14	45

404 Total passing yards for Aaron Rodgers; he also threw four TDs

yards to James Jones to put Green Bay up 14–0.

But the Giants responded with two scores of their own, including an 85-yard scoring pass from quarterback Eli Manning to Mario Manningham.

In the waning minutes of the first half, though, the Packers put another drive together, going from their own 21 in six plays and scoring on an eight-yard pass from Rodgers to John Kuhn.

The Packers then did what a desperate team is supposed to do. In the second half, they took control of a game that the Giants weren't sure they really wanted.

On the third play of the third quarter, Charles Woodson forced a fumble that safety Atari Bigby recovered. It resulted in a 31-yard Mason Crosby field goal. After a Giants field goal, Rodgers hit back-to-back passes of 33 yards to Donald Driver and 36 to Greg Jennings that

The Packers defense swarms the Giants' Ahmad Bradshaw. New York's leading rusher was limited to just 31 yards on 12 carries, a dismal 2.6 yards-per-carry average.

eventually led to a Rodgers touchdown pass to tight end Donald Lee.

The rout was on.

Manning threw interceptions on two straight series—one to Nick Collins and the other to Sam Shields—and both resulted in Packers' touchdowns by John Kuhn, who was rapidly become a fan favorite. Every time he touched the ball, fans screamed "Kooooon" in honor of the free agent who battled his way onto the roster.

"It's pretty funny," said Kuhn, who spent a year on the Pittsburgh Steelers roster and actually earned a Super Bowl ring two years ago. "I don't want to disappoint them."

The Packers earned a thunderous victory, as the defense forced six turnovers, including intercepting Manning four times. It was the kind of thumping that had the Giants questioning themselves.

"We came out and played like we didn't have any-thing to play for," Giants defensive end Justin Tuck said.

Rodgers, a week after sitting out with a concussion, was impeccable, completing 25 of 37 passes for a season-high 404 yards and four touchdowns. The major benefac-tors of those throws were Jennings, who caught seven for 142 yards and Nelson, who finished with four catches for 124 yards.

It was the kind of performance coach Mike McCarthy had hoped to see from a team that knew what was at stake and played like it. "Those guys were ready to play," he said. "They were sick and tired of hearing how tough the Giants were all week."

Now the math was even simpler. If the Packers beat the Bears the following Sunday in the season finale at Lambeau, they were playoff-bound.

"We're going to do the same thing next week," a confident Collins declared. ■

(above) Tramon Williams expertly breaks up this Eli Manning pass heading towards Mario Manningham. Manning threw for 300 yards but his four interceptions may have doomed the Giants' playoff hopes. (right) Aaron Rodgers raises his arms in celebration as John Kuhn carries in from eight yards out. The Packers were halfway through their win-and-in gauntlet to end the season.

Bear-ly Enough

January 2, 2011 • Lambeau Field, Green Bay, Wisconsin

So here it was. The final game of a season that had featured more twists and turns than anyone could have imagined. There were no subtle permutations, no weird NFL tie-breaker rules to interpret. There would be no controversy and no question about what would happen and how things would shake out.

If the Green Bay Packers beat the Chicago Bears, they would grab the final NFC wild-card playoff berth and keep playing the following week. If they lost to the Bears, they'd have to hope the Giants lost their final game to Washington Redskins (which they did not).

The Bears, champs of the NFC North, had a first-round playoff bye no matter what, but they did not plan to make life easy for the Packers. Many teams already set in the playoffs might have chosen to rest at least some of their starters to avoid needless injury. Not the Bears and certainly not against the Packers.

"Everyone will play," said Bears coach Lovie Smith, whose first order of business when he took over in Chicago seven years earlier was to consistently beat the Packers. And with everything the Packers had dealt with during this season, why would they expect anything less?

Maybe because of what was at stake or maybe because of the opponent, there was a different feel to this game than there was the week before against the Giants. More tension. More uncertainty. More of a feeling that one mistake could be costly.

The Packers could get nothing going offensively in

Packers 10, Bears 3

	1	2	3	4	F
CHI	0	3	0	0	3
GB	0	0	3	7	10

6 The number of times the Packers defense sacked Jay Cutler, with the win making the Packers the sixth seed in the NFC playoffs

the first half. Indeed, the only real threat Green Bay could muster ended at the Bears' 43 when Donald Driver fumbled after a reception.

The Bears were hardly any better. Their only score of the half (and the game) came on a nice drive in which they had a first and goal and Packers' 4-yard line. But a first down run netted nothing, a second down pass fell incomplete, and on third down quarterback Jay Cutler was sacked. That resulted in a Robbie Gould field goal and 3–0 Bears' halftime lead.

The Packers continued to struggle offensively in the second half and perhaps began to realize that if they were going to win, it might have to be the defense that carried the day. And Dom Capers' unit did just that midway through the quarter when backup cornerback Charlie Peprah intercepted a Cutler pass in the end zone to snuff out a drive.

Jay Cutler is brought down by a blitzing Packer—a sight that was to become all too familiar for Chicago fans over the last weeks of the season. This time, it was A.J. Hawk (50) harassing Cutler, with help from Jarius Wynn (94).

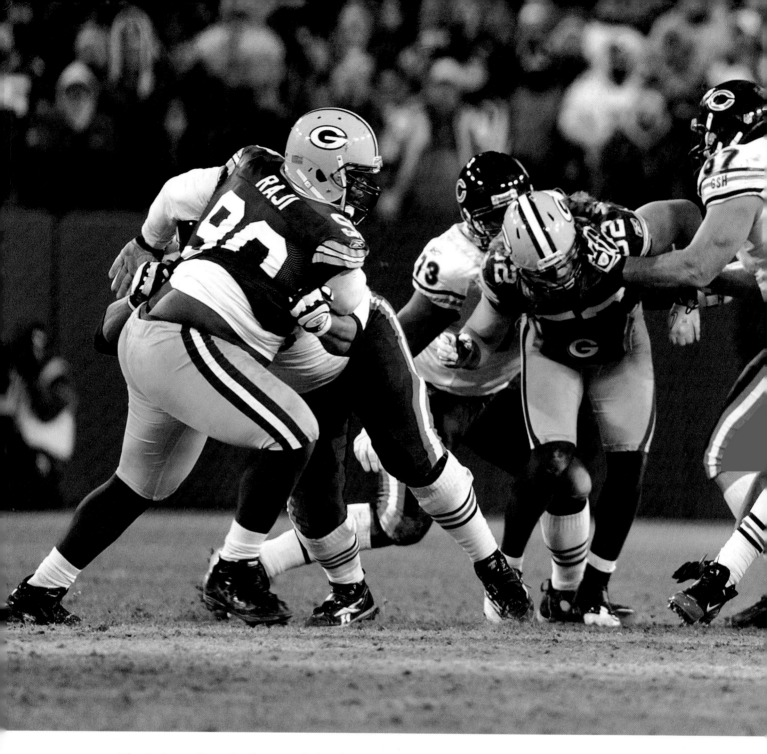

The Packers offense finally responded with a drive highlighted by a 33-yard pass from Aaron Rodgers to Greg Jennings that resulted in a Mason Crosby field goal.

Finally, in the early minutes of the fourth quarter, Green Bay clawed out a touchdown. Rodgers connected for 46 yards to Jennings down to the Bears' 1. On the next play, Rodgers found Donald Lee for the go-ahead score.

Now it was up to the Packers defense and the unit responded to the challenge.

The Packers sacked Cutler twice and as he drove the Bears from his own 2 to the Packers 32 in the final minute of the game, Nick Collins stepped up with an interception to seal the win.

The Packers were nothing special offensively, managing

Chicago's Jay Cutler could run, but he couldn't hide from the swarming Green Bay defense. On this play, B.J. Raji (90), Clay Matthews (52), and Jarius Wynn (94) gave the Bears' blockers more than they could handle.

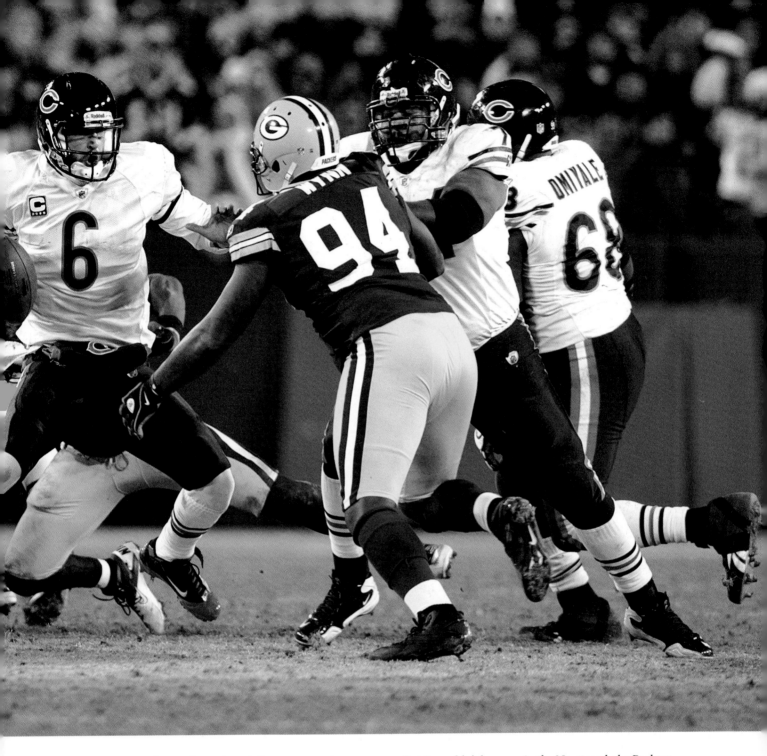

just 284 total yards. But the Packers defense was even better, allowing the Bears just 227 yards. It was a championship effort when the Packers needed it most.

Now, everyone was even.

"Those guys told us during the game that they didn't want to see us in [the playoffs]," Driver said. "That tells you how much people are scared of us. Now they have to face us."

But it wouldn't be easy. As the No. 6 seed, the Packers would have to travel for as long as they kept winning. But for a Packers team that endured so much during the season that was just fine. It was the playoffs, after all, and anything could happen.

Couldn't it? ∎

Pass-Catchers

Driver Leads Talented Receiving Corps

Who are those guys? For the better part of two seasons, when the talk focused on the Green Bay Packers and their sublime offense, it was invariably a conversation about quarterback Aaron Rodgers and that stable of wide receivers.

But while everyone seems to understand that the Packers have a few guys who can catch the ball and run a long way with it, who really knows the individual parts?

For the record, the cast of characters is as diverse as any the NFL has ever seen. By themselves, none is a breakout star, but as a collective, they are a multi-headed force that can damage defenses in a thousand different ways.

The dean of the receiving corps is Donald Driver, now in his 12th season out of Alcorn State. He came to Green Bay as a seventh-round draft project from the fertile mind of general manager Ron Wolf. More a track star than anything (he high-jumped 7'6" in college), by sheer determination Driver made himself into a top-notch receiver. He is now, incredibly, the Packers' all-time leading receiver with 698 receptions, 9,615 yards, and 53 touchdowns.

He is the closest tie to the old days, drafted in 1999, a year after the Packers last Super Bowl trip to San Diego in 1998. "This is what you dream of," Driver said after the Packers beat the Chicago Bears for the NFC title.

His story is especially compelling because of his background growing up in Houston, Texas. Desperately poor,

he survived at times by selling drugs and living under a Houston overpass when things were especially difficult.

Now Driver is the face of the Packers organization, inheriting an annual charity softball game that was started by Brett Favre and giving back whenever and wherever he can.

Time and injury have made Driver more of a possession receiver than a deep threat these days. Still, he remains a major offensive force. Just ask the San Francisco 49ers, who on Week 13 watched Driver take a short pass, break at least seven tackles, and score on a scintillating 61-yard play.

The Packers' deep threat is fifth-year man Greg Jennings from Western Michigan. Irrepressible and mercurial, Jennings can score from anywhere on the field. He was the Packers leading receiver in 2010 with 76 receptions for 1,265 yards and team-high 12 touchdowns. He has already caught 322 passes and scored 40 touchdowns in his career and, if he stays healthy, he could eclipse Driver as the Packers' all-time receiving leader.

James Jones, in his fourth season from San Jose State, was Green Bay's third-leading receiver with 50 catches for 679 yards and five scores. Jones remains an enigma, a receiver capable of making impossible catches while occasionally dropping the easy one.

The No. 4 guy is Jordy Nelson, who in 2008 was the Packers' first draft choice (as the fifth pick in the second

The Packers pass-catching trio of (left to right) Jordy Nelson, Greg Jennings, and Donald Driver celebrate an early season touchdown reception by Jennings.

round). Solid, unspectacular, he just makes play when they need to be made.

Perhaps nowhere was Nelson more important than in the late-game loss to the Atlanta Falcons, when he straddled the sideline in the end zone to catch a rocket thrown by Rodgers in the final minute to tie the game. The play would have been far more celebrated if the Packers had won. Instead, it was just another example of what Nelson can do when he's needed.

Then there are the tight ends. Jermichael Finley is the athletic freak. Tall, strong, and speedy, if he can stay healthy he just might redefine the tight end position in the NFL.

When Finley went down midway through the season, three guys filled his role—rookie Andrew Quarless, vet-

eran Donald Lee, and free agent Tom Crabtree. They combined for 36 receptions and six touchdowns. Crabtree, unknown and unexpected, caught his first touchdown as a pro as the Packers took a 7–0 lead on the Eagles in the postseason opener.

"How about that?" Crabtree said afterward. "Who would've expected that?"

It is an interesting, diverse, and dangerous bunch who make up the Packers receiving corps and coach Mike McCarthy found a way to get all of them involved in one form or another. Perhaps out of necessity because of their crippled running game, the Packers may have revolutionized how to use receivers in the NFL.

"We're all out here for each other," Jennings. "When one of us succeeds, we all succeed." ■

(above) Jermichael Finley catches a pass during the first half of the Bills game. (opposite) Greg Jennings looks the ball into his hands during training camp 2010. The ensuing season was the best of his five-year career. After a slow start, he amassed 76 receptions, 1,265 yards, and 12 touchdowns.

Philly's Finale

January 9, 2011 • Lincoln Financial Field, Philadelphia, Pennsylvania

It was a mixture of relief, satisfaction, and joy that accompanied the Green Bay Packers as they prepared for their NFC Wild Card playoff game against the Philadelphia Eagles. But in truth these Packers had been in playoff mode for the better part of a month anyway. After back-to-back losses to the Detroit Lions and New England Patriots in mid-December, the Packers knew what they had to do: win or go home, which sounds an awful lot like a playoff game scenario.

So it was into that pressure-packed cauldron the Packers entered the final two weeks of the regular season. They responded with an easy win over the New York Giants and a tough win over the Chicago Bears. So if any team was playoff tested, it was the Packers.

Their first-round foe would be a familiar one. The Packers and Eagles had faced off in the season's opening week, but a lot had changed for both teams since that early September afternoon.

Green Bay had, of course, absorbed a ton of key injuries, ultimately putting 16 players on injured reserve. The offense had found its stride, and the defense, which had seemed so confounded by the entrance of Michael Vick in that first Philadelphia game, was playing with confidence and speed.

The Eagles, of course, had committed to Vick and he had responded with an MVP-type season.

Packers 21, Eagles 16

	1	2	3	4	F
GB	7	7	7	0	21
PHI	0	3	7	6	16

123 Total net rushing yards for James Starks, in 23 attempts

But while Vick ran through, over, and past the Packers the first time they met, Packers' defensive coordinator Dom Capers this time had a week to prepare and a season's worth of tape to watch in anticipation. It would make a difference.

Offensively, coach Mike McCarthy came out with a new look against the blitzing, aggressive Eagles defense. He used personnel groupings he hadn't used before. He ran motions he hadn't unveiled before. He used a variation of the wishbone backfield, which utilized John Kuhn at fullback and Brandon Jackson and James Starks as the halfbacks.

McCarthy brilliantly countered Philly's aggressiveness on defense with aggressiveness of his own on offense.

In the face of Philadelphia pressure, Aaron Rodgers dumps off a short throw to John Kuhn. The sturdy running back caught three passes for 33 yards.

It was a master stroke.

And perhaps most important, when he saw Starks break off a 27-yard run on his first carry of the game midway through the first quarter, McCarthy decided that was a horse he had to ride.

Starks, who had run well earlier in the season against the 49ers, had found his place in McCarthy's doghouse with poor practice habits after that. Now he was getting another chance he didn't plan to blow it.

Keeping the Eagles off-balance, the Packers built a 14–0 lead in the second quarter on touchdown passes from Aaron Rodgers to backup tight end Tom Crabtree and James Jones.

Still leading 14–3 in the waning seconds of the first half, the Packers could have put a dagger in the Eagles as Rodgers hit Jones perfectly in stride for what should have been a 63-yard touchdown. But Jones dropped the ball.

On the heels of this reprieve, Philadelphia rallied in the third quarter. Rodgers fumbled away the ball after being sacked, and Vick connected with Jason Avant for a 24-yard touchdown.

(above) Mike Vick may have been an MVP front runner in 2010, but he was battered all day by the Packers' defense. Here, Erik Walden drops the Philadelphia signal-caller. (right) James Starks breaks into the Philadelphia secondary. He led all rushers with 123 yards on the ground, averaging more than five yards per carry in the best game of his young career.

Perhaps in previous seasons, that turn of fortune might have crippled the Packers. Not this year. Rodgers came right back with a 10-play, 80-yard drive capped by a perfect screen pass to Jackson for the score.

Then it was survival time. Vick's fourth-quarter, fourth-down touchdown sneak cut the Green Bay lead 21–16 and it stayed that way after a failed two-point conversion.

Philly had one final drive and moved from its own 34 to the Packers' 27 in five plays before Vick's pass to the end zone was intercepted by Tramon Williams to end the game.

"I felt I got greedy and I took a shot at the end zone," Vick said later. "You learn from that."

For Rodgers, it was another solid effort as he completed 18 of 27 passes for 180 yards and three scores. It was also Rodgers' first playoff win as Green Bay's quarter-back, a fact brought up by many in the media.

"I never felt I had a monkey on my back," Rodgers relied. "It was just good to win."

Starks was the real surprise as he roared for 123 yards on 23 carries and offered the Packers some badly needed balance.

It was a good start, but now the Packers had a bigger task—traveling back to the Georgia Dome for a rematch with the top-seeded Falcons. ∎

(above) Packers' long snapper Brett Goode prepares to deliver the ball to punter Tim Masthay during the game against the Eagles. (opposite) James Jones and Aaron Rodgers react after their second-quarter touchdown hookup gave Green Bay the lead for good.

Dome-ination

January 15, 2011 • Georgia Dome, Atlanta, Georgia

What's the phrase? A mile wide and an inch deep? Perhaps that was the best way to describe the Atlanta Falcons' confidence as they prepared for their Divisional Playoff game against the now-very-dangerous Green bay Packers.

The Falcons had constructed a very nice regular season. Behind quarterback Matt "Matty Ice" Ryan, dynamic wide receiver Roddy White, and a solid if unspectacular defense, the Falcons had claimed the NFC's top seed with an impressive 13–3 record, including a 7–1 home record in the Georgia Dome.

They had already beaten the Packers once, an entertaining 20–17 November victory in Atlanta at which time White had proclaimed, "We don't want to go to Lambeau in January. We want them to come here."

The Falcons were confident and rested and talking about how ready they were to take the next step forward. They talked with a swagger that was not earned—at least not yet. This was, after all, still a franchise that didn't have the history, the pedigree to build on. There were no Super Bowl titles just yet.

The Packers, on the other hand, had been in crisis mode for a month. They won three straight games they had to win, including a mugging on the road of the always-dangerous Eagles the previous week. Green Bay knew it would have no more home games, so the team hunkered down and prepared to do what it needed to do.

In front of a deafening crowd at the Georgia Dome,

Packers 48, Falcons 21

	1	2	3	4	F
GB	0	28	14	6	48
ATL	7	7	0	7	21

35 Consecutive points scored by the Packers as Aaron Rodgers completed 31 of 36 pass for 366 yards and three TDs

the Falcons did indeed strike first, forcing a Greg Jennings fumble on the Packers' third play from scrimmage and converting the turnover into a 12-yard Michael Turner touchdown run.

But by the second quarter, the Packers had settled in. Led by Aaron Rodgers and rapidly improving cornerback Tramon Williams, Green Bay buried the Falcons and their championship hopes.

Rodgers first threw a touchdown pass to Jordy Nelson to tie the game at 7–7. But on the next kickoff, Atlanta's Eric Weems electrified the crowd again with a 102-yard return for the longest postseason touchdown in NFL history.

Green Bay was undaunted because, well, they'd been here before. Rodgers' response was a 10-play, 92-yard drive capped by a 1-yard touchdown run by John Kuhn.

Aaron Rodgers scans downfield for an open receiver in the second half against the Falcons. It was perhaps Rodgers' best day as a pro as well as the best postseason performance by a Packers' quarterback.

Williams followed with an interception of Ryan in the Packers' end zone and Rodgers came back the other way, driving another 80 yards and hitting James Jones for the touchdown.

Then came the crushing blow for the Falcons.

As Ryan was trying to drive his team into field goal range in the final seconds of the first half, he threw an out pattern read perfectly by Williams. He intercepted it and returned the pick 70 yards for the touchdown and a 28–14 Packers lead at halftime.

The Georgia Dome was as quiet as a tomb.

"I probably shouldn't have thrown that," Ryan said simply after the game.

The Packers kept it going in the second half as Rodgers played about as close to a perfect game as a quarterback could play.

He ran for one touchdown in the third quarter and threw to Kuhn for another, and the win turned into a rout.

By the end of the game, the three-quarters empty stadium belonged to Packers fans who chanted "Go, Pack, Go" through most of the final 15 minutes.

Rodgers' numbers were borderline unbelievable. He completed 31 of 36 passes for 366 yards and three scores. He eluded tacklers; he made pinpoint throws; he did everything he was supposed to do—and more

"This was probably my best performance," he admitted after the game. "The stage we were on and the importance of the game. It was a good night. I felt like I was in a zone."

The Packers dominated the Falcons in all aspects of the game, rolling up 442 yards in offense and holding the Falcons to 194.

Meanwhile, the Falcons had received another harsh lesson about the difference between regular-season football and playoff football. "We will learn from this," said coach Mike Smith. "That's the important thing."

For the Packers, it was two down and one to go. They knew their rivals, the Bears, were playing the next day against the upstart Seattle Seahawks, and while none of the players professed to care who won, they cared. A lot.

The Packers wanted the Bears. ■

B.J. Raji is a week away from being a hero for his defensive prowess, but against the Falcons he celebrates his blocking skills: inserted as a fullback, he blasted a hole for John Kuhn's (30) second-quarter touchdown plunge.

Aaron Rodgers lithely steps around the diving tackle of Curtis Lofton on his seven-yard third-quarter touchdown scramble.

On to Dallas

January 23, 2011 • Soldier Field, Chicago, Illinois

In some corner of their minds, the Green Bay players probably knew it would come down to this. Through everything they had dealt with—the inconsistency, the injuries, and the uncertainty—the Packers held firm to the belief that they were good enough to play for the NFC Championship.

They had won four straight games they were required to win, including the last two on the road against teams geared to stop them.

They were on one of the surreal magic rides they had seen other teams latch onto. And while they didn't quite understand it, they had no intention of getting off anytime soon. This was epic, once-in-a-career stuff.

And now it was laid out for them: The Packers would travel back to Chicago to take on the Bears. A win meant a trip to the Super Bowl. A loss and all that hard work came to nothing.

The hype during the week leading up to the game was unprecedented for the NFL's oldest and sometimes most-heated rivalry. Green Bay and Chicago had not met in a playoff game since 1941. This was the biggest Packers-Bears game of all time.

The Packers wasted no time in trying to quiet the boisterous—and cold—Soldier Field crowd, moving the ball at will during the game's first drive. Two long completions to Greg Jennings set up an Aaron Rodgers 1-yard touchdown run for a quick 7–0 lead.

Packers 21, Bears 14

	1	2	3	4	F
GB	7	7	0	7	21
CHI	0	0	0	14	14

18

Yardage of the fourth-quarter interception return for a touchdown by 337-lb. nose tackle B.J. Raji

At the start of the second quarter, the Packers rolled again, moving 44 yards on five plays and scoring on a James Starks lunge into the end zone.

It could have—and should have—been worse for the Bears later in the quarter, but Donald Driver let a Rodgers pass slip through his hands and linebacker Lance Briggs was there for the interception. The Bears had done nothing on offense, the Packers had dominated, and yet Green Bay led just 14–0 at halftime.

What the Packers—and apparently a few Bears—didn't know was that Jay Cutler had injured his left knee while being sacked in the second quarter. He tried to play in the first series of the third quarter but could not. He took a seat and backup Todd Collins took over.

The Packers threatened to take what could have been

Sam Shields ends a Bears' threat at the end of the first half by intercepting this Jay Cutler pass. Shields sealed the win with his second interception, a fourth-down pick of Caleb Hanie in the game's final seconds.

an insurmountable lead early in the third quarter. But an ill-advised Rodgers pass near the Bears' goal line was intercepted by linebacker Brian Urlacher. He would have taken it back for a touchdown, too, if not for Rodgers' heads-up tackle.

"I don't get paid to make tackles but that was probably one of my best plays of the day," Rodgers said with a smile.

Yet the Bears could do nothing with the gift. Two series, two failures, and Bears head coach Lovie Smith had seen enough of Collins. He inserted his No. 3 quarterback, the unknown Caleb Hanie, and something special happened.

Hanie directed the Bears on an eight-play, 67-yard

drive that ended with a Chester Taylor touchdown run with 12 minutes left in the game. The momentum had shifted Chicago's way.

Then with just over six minutes to play, Hanie, who played calmly and with purpose, made a critical mistake when he threw an interception to Packers' nose tackle B.J. Raji, who rumbled 18 yards for a touchdown and a 21–7 Green Bay lead.

Game over? Not yet. Hanie came right back, hit Earl Bennett on a 35-yard score and, it was a one-touchdown game with plenty of time left.

When Green Bay failed to move the ball on its next

(above) The Bears secondary gives chase but can't track down Aaron Rodgers as he sprints to the end zone. (right) Brandon Jackson looks for daylight on a 16-yard reception out of the backfield.

possession, Hanie directed yet another impressive drive, moving the Bears from their own 29 to the Green Bay 29 with less than a minute to play. But before Hanie could complete the miracle comeback, rookie Sam Shields saved the day for Packers with his second interception of the game.

It was over. The Packers were headed to the Super Bowl.

"I'm at a loss for words," said Rodgers, who threw for 244 yards and ran for another 39.

When it mattered most, the Packers defense made the play it needed to make. Green Bay was back in the Super Bowl for the first time since 1998.

"We just kept playing defense the way we know how to play it," said linebacker Clay Matthews.

The opponent? The Packers didn't know at that stage but they also didn't care. They had gone on the road and won three playoffs games against teams they had lost to during the regular season.

It had been an incredible season. And the best part was, it wasn't over. ■

(above) Tim Masthay had no problems with the notorious poor footing and swirling winds at Soldier Field. His superior punting minimized the return threat of the dangerous Devin Hester. (opposite) James Starks eludes a Brian Urlacher tackle on this play, but he had a tough day running, gaining just 22 yards.

Nose tackle B.J. Raji dances into the end zone with what would prove to be the game-winning touchdown. His 18-yard interception return of a Caleb Hanie pass was the key play in fending off the Bears' furious fourth-quarter comeback.

Charles Woodson lifts the new George Halas Trophy, awarded to the NFC Champions, after the Packers beat the Bears 21–14 to earn a spot in Super Bowl XLV.